Audrey Ellis, famous author of more
than fifty practical and imaginative
cookery books, including many on the
subject of home freezing, also frequently
acts as food advisor to programmes for
Thames Television and London
Weekend Television. A former
Managing Editor of cookery books for a
major publishing group, she now
contributes regularly to three national
magazines as well as continuing to
produce more titles to add to her
formidable list of books.

Mrs Ellis travels widely, has a second
home in California and often visits
relatives in France.

The Great Little Cookbook

All you need to know
about cooking in one
book.

Audrey Ellis

CORGI BOOKS
A DIVISION OF TRANSWORLD PUBLISHERS LTD

THE GREAT LITTLE COOKBOOK
A CORGI BOOK 0 552 11912 1

First publication in Great Britain

PRINTING HISTORY
Corgi edition published 1982
Corgi edition 'P' reprinted 1982

Copyright © Audrey Ellis 1982

This book is set in 10/11 pt Plantin

Corgi Books are published by
Transworld Publishers Ltd.,
Century House, 61-63 Uxbridge Road,
Ealing, London, W5 5SA

Made and printed in Great Britain by
Hunt Barnard Printing Ltd., Aylesbury, Bucks.

CONTENTS

INTRODUCTION

In my experience, cookbooks often provide a huge choice of recipes, the majority of which are thumbed through and never used. This may be because the ingredients are too expensive, the method is too complicated or simply that the necessary equipment is not available. Here is a book that takes a totally new approach to cooking. I believe that it fills the modern need for a streamlined collection of reliable recipes using the latest time-saving techniques. These are clearly described, and used to prepare the food most people today find healthy and enjoyable, for a reasonable outlay. The minimum number of utensils is needed — so you will not have to face a mountain of washing-up after preparing a meal. My basic recipes are frequently made more valuable by the introduction of exciting variations. This should encourage you to build up a repertoire of favourite dishes you could hardly hope to find in a book twice this size. Where an ingredient such as a made-up sauce or herbed butter is mentioned, it is marked with an asterisk, meaning that the recipe appears elsewhere in the book. Even if you have previously done little cooking, with the help of my recipes your prowess in the kitchen will soon increase and bring you great satisfaction.

CHOOSING EQUIPMENT

You may have no choice in whether you cook by gas, electricity or solid fuel, but generally speaking beginners at cookery find it easiest to cook with gas. You can see and judge adjustments to the heat source instantly. If a new installation is possible, consider having a gas hob and an electric oven and make sure the oven has stay-clean lining. If you opt for a split level arrangement, insist on having the oven installed at a height which is convenient for you to use, whatever the conventional housing offered by the makers of the kitchen units. If you are tall, a high level oven may suit you, although a cook who is petite would struggle dangerously to remove heavy roasting tins and casseroles from a level well above her waist. A refrigerator installed under a working surface often provides a much-needed working area above but for a tall person this entails constant stooping and crouching to see what is inside the refrigerator. Do 'go through the motions' of using the big pieces of kitchen equipment before you purchase them, remembering that shop displays usually imply impossibly large kitchens or, at the most, only show you two adjacent walls. Wipe-clean working surfaces are standard these days but when you must choose between such luxuries as a double sink with waste disposer in one of them or a dishwasher, your lifestyle must be the deciding factor. Couples who are usually only washing up for two, and whose kitchen waste has to be carried some distance to a dustbin, might find the waste disposer more truly labour-saving than the dishwasher.

Major pieces of equipment now extend beyond hob, oven and refrigerator. Here are some comments on other items you might be considering.

Microwave Cooker
The cooker should be free standing. Since it plugs in anywhere

to a 13-amp socket, its portability is an added bonus. Modern domestic microwave cookers are *safe* and very helpful in defrosting and subsequently cooking many kinds of frozen food. They do not, in my opinion, represent a substitute for a conventional cooker. But the advantage to a busy cook of being able to defrost an average roasting chicken in 25 minutes and cook it in another 25 minutes must be considerable. When choosing, make sure the model provides two power levels, one for defrosting and one for cooking, and a turntable.

Multicooker
This table-top piece of equipment requires only a 13-amp socket and performs many functions. It has the initial advantage of thermostatically controlled temperature, can be used open or covered with the domed lid which has an optional vent, and even comes provided with a ceramic liner which converts it to a slow electric cooker. The capacity is generous enough to cook a complete main meal for four people; but you can use it to steam puddings and bake cakes.

Slow Electric Cooker
This is a similar piece of equipment which plugs into a 13-amp socket. It is ideal for a housewife who is absent at work all day, or for anyone else who cannot be sure to return at exactly the time by which a meal will be cooked. The slow cooking method allows considerable flexibility and enables you to use the cheaper cuts of meat to good advantage. You can also cook puddings in it, but they can usually only be left unattended for 5 hours at the most. I have found that the addition of liquid must be carefully controlled as dishes cooked by this method tend to produce more moisture than one would expect.

Pressure Cooker
The introduction of an automatic pressure cooker which obviates the necessity to judge reduction of pressure yourself and to hold a heavy piece of equipment under running water, etc. makes it more attractive as an investment. It cooks quickly at a higher temperature than is possible under normal atmospheric pressure.

Wok
This indispensable cooking utensil for the Chinese is becoming
very popular here because it is ideally adapted for the stir-frying
method. Quick cooking of thinly sliced raw food retains nutri-
tional value and saves fuel. Food can be prepared in advance and
freshly cooked in a few minutes when needed. There is only one
pan to wash up and a wok holds plenty so you can cook enough
in it to serve 4 people generously. One point which may be overlooked is that the wok does not sit flat on top of our western
stoves. You need a special ring to hold it steady while you are
cooking.

Waterless Pan
A specially bonded metal sandwiched between layers of stainless steel produces a pan which distributes heat so that food can
be cooked covered over very low heat almost without any added
liquid without burning, and still remain moist; although in the
case of vegetables, only the water adhering to them after washing need be used. The lid forms a suction seal so that the pressure inside the pan is *lower* than normal atmospheric pressure.
Far less salt is needed than when cooking by the conventional
method and no valuable nutrients are wasted by being thrown
away in cooking water.

Griddle or Girdle
Although you can use a solid hot-plate on an electric cooker provided it has been well cleaned, heavy metal griddles are available to be placed over either gas or electric heat, preferably a
radiant ring. Lightly greased, they are ideal for cooking drop-
scones, bacon and eggs and other quick snacks. (A heavy-duty
frying pan can often be used as a substitute.)

WORTHWHILE GADGETS AND UTENSILS

To carry out automatically almost all preparation processes in
cooking, there is no aid to equal the food processor. It mixes,
blends, liquidises, slices, chops, minces, chips, grates. Invest in

one if you possibly can. If you cannot, an electric handmixer and blender will take over most of these jobs, but you will probably also need a hand-operated chopper, mincer and mandoline for fine slicing. A hand grater for such jobs as removing the rind from citrus fruit is an essential extra in any case. Other pieces of electrical equipment which are frequently useful (some alas are not) are a sandwich toaster, yogurt maker, and electric carving knife. If your cooker does not possess a handy grill for making toast, an electric toaster is helpful, but check the aperture to make sure it will take the size and shape of bread slice you favour. A wall-mounted can opener, not necessarily electric, is much more efficient than a hand-held one.

Among indispensable tools for your kitchen are − potato peeler (useful for peeling other vegetables and some fruit), apple corer, wire whisk, knife sharpener, measuring spoons and jugs, ladle, potato masher and slotted draining spoons. These items are often overlooked when stocking up with non-essentials like biscuit cutters (which can be replaced by using the tops of glasses of different sizes) and a rolling pin (which can be replaced by using a milk bottle). Such specialised tools as a melon baller, butter curler and canelling knife can be added when ideas for small presents are required. A colander, sieves and strainers of various sizes are often needed. The nylon type is ideal for straining hot and cold liquids but not hot oil. Remember also that you cannot dip pastry brushes into hot oil without ruining them and this applies also to boiling glazes which contain oil. A few more unusual items which can be invaluable are the hanging spoon measure for small weights and the jug scale for measuring small quantities of both dry and liquid foods.

Knives
Stainless steel knives, which never discolour and rarely need professional sharpening, are recommended. The smaller sizes seem to be used more often than the large ones and some with serrated edges should be included, plus a curved grapefruit knife. Be sure you have at least one carving fork with a guard.

12

THE NON-STICK REVOLUTION

The new bonded non-stick surfaces on pans and baking tins of all descriptions are far more robust and therefore permanent than the early non-stick surfaces, which tended to scrape off and disappear after little use. With a moderate amount of care and wherever possible using plastic-coated or wooden utensils, non-stick cookware will give you years of faithful use and there are three major advantages:

1 Very much less fat is needed for frying and indeed you can actually 'dry fry' an egg without any fat at all.
2 Food which used to stick during cooking can easily be removed.
3 Washing-up is reduced to a minimum. Often it can be replaced by wiping out the pan carefully with absorbent kitchen paper.

SOLID MEASURES USING SPOONS AND CUPS

This chart provides useful approximate equivalents to 25 g (1 oz).

	TABLESPOONS	U.S. CUPS
Breadcrumbs (dry)	6	$\frac{1}{4}$ cup
Breadcrumbs (fresh)	7	$\frac{1}{2}$ cup
Butter	$1\frac{1}{2}$	$\frac{1}{8}$ cup (2 U.S. tablespoons)
Cornflour	2	$\frac{1}{4}$ cup cornstarch
Flour	3	$\frac{1}{4}$ cup sifted
Rice	2	$\frac{1}{8}$ cup
Sugar (castor)	2	$\frac{1}{8}$ cup granulated
Sugar (demerara)	2	$\frac{1}{8}$ cup, brown, firmly packed
Sugar (icing)	4	$\frac{1}{4}$ cup, confectioner's, sifted

3 teaspoons equal 1 tablespoon

LIQUID MEASURES USING SPOONS AND CUPS

2 tablespoons = about 30 ml (1 fl oz)
1 teaspoon = about 5 ml
1 tablespoon = about 15 ml
8 tablespoons = about 150 ml ($\frac{1}{4}$ pint)
250 ml (8 fl oz) = 1 U.S. cup
3 teaspoons = 1 tablespoon

BOTTLE SIZES

Standard wine bottle = 700–750 ml (about $1\frac{1}{3}$ pints) ($3\frac{1}{4}$ U.S. cups)
Litre bottle = $1\frac{3}{4}$ pints ($4\frac{1}{3}$ U.S. cups)
Miniature bottle = about 30–45 ml (2–3 tablespoons)
Two litre bottle = $3\frac{1}{2}$ pints ($8\frac{2}{3}$ U.S. cups)

OVEN TEMPERATURE CHART

Description	°Celcius	°Fahrenheit	Gas Mark
Very cool	110	225	$\frac{1}{4}$
	120	250	$\frac{1}{2}$
Cool	140	275	1
	150	300	2
Moderate	160	325	3
	180	350	4
Moderately Hot	190	375	5
	200	400	6
Hot	220	425	7
	230	450	8
Very Hot	240	475	9

IMPROVISATION OF EQUIPMENT

Some items you would rarely use may not be worth purchasing, especially if they are expensive ones. Every-day utensils can often be used to take their place.

BAIN MARIE − Stand the dish containing the food to be cooked in a roasting tin and pour in water to come half-way up the sides. Cook in the oven.

DOUBLE BOILER − Place the food to be cooked in a basin and put this over a pan of hot, simmering or boiling water, according to the recipe.

OVENPROOF DISHES − Foil containers are very useful and come in many sizes and shapes. Depending on the food to be cooked it may be necessary to use one container inside another for firmness, or to place the container on a baking sheet for cooking.

FLOUR/SUGAR SIFTER − Choose a container with lid and punch holes in the top.

CONFUSING COOKERY TERMS EXPLAINED

Whisking is a brisk action for incorporating air into foods such as egg whites or cream, or combining ingredients probably for a sauce or dressing. Beating is generally carried out with a wooden spoon and is intended to combine foods and eliminate lumps in mixtures such as cake batters. To *sauté* means to fry foods in a little fat over high heat, tossing and turning them until golden brown all over. Stir-frying is a process frequently used in Chinese-type cookery. Small pieces or thin slices of food are literally stirred while being fried in very little oil until tender. Another bewildering French cookery term is *gratin*. This is usually interpreted as meaning finished under the grill and probably sprinkled with cheese. In fact, it means coated with breadcrumbs and may as well be finished in the oven as under the grill. The term *mornay* does indicate a dish including a cheese sauce.

RECIPE SECTION

The methods introduced in the following recipes are, in every case, those which are simplest to use and yet sure to produce successful results. Many of the recipes themselves contain suggested variations, but having practised the simple preparation steps needed, you can invent other variations yourself.

My aim has been to provide you with a repertoire of cooking techniques, not requiring an enormous range of utensils and equipment, which yet make truly adventurous cooking possible. Certain classic recipes, such as one for puff pastry, have been omitted because the ready-made product is so excellent.

One golden rule – do not skimp the time you spend on reading a recipe through before you begin or on the instructions supplied with a new piece of equipment. Look after the kitchen utensils that serve you well. Put each item away carefully, so that one does not damage another, and in a state where they are absolutely ready for the next time you want to use them. For example, tighten a loose handle on a pan as soon as you notice it, and if a knife seems to have lost some of its cutting edge, sharpen it immediately. Time is well spent occasionally checking through your food stocks, throwing away empty packets and noting down items that need to be replaced. If your cupboards and drawers are in confusion it takes you twice as long to get ready to cook.

Finally, pay as much attention to the presentation of food as the cooking of it. Just as young red wines benefit immensely from being opened and left in a warm place some hours before drinking, and white wine from being briefly chilled in advance, so does food benefit from the little touches you add at serving time. Chopped parsley, watercress sprigs, lemon slices or a dash of paprika pepper on a colourless dish are invaluable aids to make food look attractive. And that's what cooking is all about; producing appetising food.

Soups and Sauces

CHILLED AVOCADO SOUP

1 large ripe avocado
Few drops of lemon juice
1 clove garlic
300 ml ($\frac{1}{2}$ pint) milk
300 ml ($\frac{1}{2}$ pint) hot chicken
  stock

Pinch of ground nutmeg
150 ml ($\frac{1}{4}$ pint) soured
  cream
Salt and pepper

Halve, stone and peel the avocado and cut 4 neat slices for the garnish. Brush these with lemon juice and keep aside. Liquidise the avocado with the remaining ingredients until smooth. Chill thoroughly and check the seasoning before serving with a slice of avocado floating on each portion in the bowl.
Serves 4.

GAZPACHO

1 medium cucumber
450 g (1 lb) ripe tomatoes
1 small green pepper,
  deseeded
1 medium onion
2 cloves garlic, chopped
3 tablespoons oil

3 tablespoons wine vinegar
450 ml ($\frac{3}{4}$ pint) tomato juice
Salt and freshly ground
  black pepper
Side dishes:
  cucumber sticks
  $\frac{1}{2}$ quantity garlic chapons*

Roughly chop the unpeeled cucumber, the tomatoes, pepper and onion. Liquidise these in small batches with the garlic, oil and vinegar. Place the mixture in a bowl, blend in the tomato juice and add salt and pepper to taste. Chill well and serve with the side dishes handed separately. (This soup is often served with ice cubes floating in it.)
Serves 4–6.

FRESH TOMATO SOUP

1 kg (2 lb) ripe tomatoes,
   peeled
2 tablespoons oil
1 large onion, chopped
1 teaspoon dried oregano
1 teaspoon dried basil

2 teaspoons Worcestershire
   sauce
Salt and pepper
1 tablespoon cornflour
450 ml ($\frac{3}{4}$ pint) chicken
   stock

Quarter the tomatoes and scoop out and discard the seeds. Heat
the oil in a medium saucepan and use to fry the onion gently
until soft but not browned. Add the tomato, herbs, Worcestershire sauce and a little seasoning. Bring to the boil, stir weil,
cover and simmer for 30 minutes, or until soft. Moisten the
cornflour with a little of the stock, add the rest to the pan and
bring back to the boil. Pour in the blended cornflour and stir
constantly until the soup boils and thickens slightly. Simmer for
a further 5 minutes and adjust the seasoning if necessary.
Serves 4–6.

Variation:

Creamy Fresh Tomato Soup – Liquidise the soup until smooth
and reheat with 150 ml ($\frac{1}{4}$ pint) single cream. Do not allow the
soup to boil.

Note: The easy way to peel tomatoes is to place them in a basin
and pour boiling water over. Leave immersed for 1 minute then
drain and the skins will slip off.

FISH CHOWDER

450 g (1 lb) white fish
   fillets
Salt and pepper
600 ml (1 pint) water
75 g (3 oz) salt belly of
   pork, derinded
2 tablespoons oil
350 g (12 oz) potatoes,
   cubed

1 large onion, chopped
1 tablespoon flour
300 ml ($\frac{1}{2}$ pint) milk
1 teaspoon lemon juice
3 tablespoons chopped
   parsley
1 quantity garlic chapons*

Place the fish in a pan with 1 teaspoon salt and the water. Bring to the boil then simmer for 10 minutes. Lift out the fish and reserve the liquid. Cut the pork into small cubes, place in a large pan and heat gently until the fat runs. Add the oil, raise the heat and continue frying until the pork bits are golden. Put in the potato and onion and fry gently, turning the pieces occasionally, until the onion is soft. Stir in the flour and when well blended gradually add the reserved liquid and the milk and bring to the boil, stirring constantly. Flake the fish and stir into the soup with the lemon juice. Season to taste with salt and pepper and simmer for 15 minutes, or until the potato is soft. Check the seasoning again, stir in the parsley and hand the chapons separately in a bowl.

Serves 4–6.

TOMATO AUBERGINE SOUP

2 tablespoons oil
1 large aubergine (about
    225 g (8 oz)), cubed
1 clove garlic, crushed
900 ml (1 $\frac{1}{2}$ pints) chicken
    or vegetable stock
2 tablespoons tomato purée

Salt and freshly ground
    black pepper
99 g (3 $\frac{1}{2}$ oz) can tuna
150 ml ($\frac{1}{4}$ pint) natural
    yogurt
Chopped parsley

Heat half the oil and use to fry half the aubergine cubes until golden. Remove them from the pan with a slotted draining spoon. Add the rest of the oil to the pan and fry the remaining aubergine cubes in the same way. Return the first batch of aubergine to the pan and add the garlic, stock, tomato purée and a little salt and pepper. Bring to the boil, cover and simmer for 15–20 minutes, or until the aubergine is tender. Flake the tuna and stir into the soup with any liquid from the can. Simmer for a further 5 minutes and adjust the seasoning if necessary. Swirl the yogurt on top of the soup and serve piping hot sprinkled with parsley.

Serves 4.

CHICKEN AND LETTUCE SOUP

4 spring onions, trimmed
25 g (1 oz) butter
1 large lettuce, shredded
2 tablespoons flour
600 ml (1 pint) milk

1 chicken portion
Salt and pepper
$\frac{1}{4}$ teaspoon dried tarragon
1 egg yolk

Chop the onions. Melt the butter in a medium pan and use to fry the onion gently for 1 minute. Add the lettuce, stir well, cover the pan and cook gently for 5 minutes. Stir in the flour and when well blended, gradually add the milk and bring to the boil, stirring constantly. Put in the chicken portion, 1 teaspoon salt, $\frac{1}{4}$ teaspoon pepper and the tarragon. Bring back to the boil, cover and simmer for 45 minutes. Lift out the chicken portion and remove the flesh from the bones and skin. Cut it into bite-sized pieces, return to the soup and bring to the boil once more. Beat the egg yolk and blend about 150 ml ($\frac{1}{4}$ pint) of the hot soup into it. Pour this mixture into the soup and stir for 1 minute. Remove from the heat and add more seasoning if necessary. Serve hot.
Serves 4.

CHICKEN VICHYSSOISE

1 large potato, grated
1 small leek, shredded
600 ml (1 pint) water
298 g (10$\frac{1}{2}$ oz) can
  condensed cream of
  chicken soup

Salt and pepper
150 ml ($\frac{1}{4}$ pint) single
  cream
2 tablespoons chopped
  chives

Place the potato, leek and water in a saucepan. Bring to the boil and cook for 10 minutes. Liquidise or sieve and blend in the soup. Taste and add seasoning if necessary. At serving time, stir in the cream. Serve hot or cold, sprinkled with the chives as a garnish.
Serves 4–6.

GARLIC CROÛTONS

2 *slices stale white bread*
1 *clove garlic*

2 *tablespoons olive or*
  corn oil

Trim the crusts from the bread and rub both sides of the slices with the cut surface of a clove of garlic. Cut into triangles. Heat the oil and when hot add the triangles and fry briskly, turning them until they are golden brown all over. Drain well and serve immediately.
Serves 4.
Variation:
Garlic Chapons – Rub the bread with garlic as above, then cut it into small dice. Add a crushed clove of garlic to the pan while frying the bread dice. Drain and sprinkle with salt. Serve with salads but do not mix with the other ingredients more than 5 minutes before serving time or the chapons will soften.
Mustard Croûtons – Cut the bread into triangles and place in a small bowl. Sift over 1 teaspoon dry mustard, shaking the bowl so that the triangles get coated evenly. Fry in oil as above until golden brown.

MEXICAN GUACAMOLE DIP

1 *large tomato*
½ *small onion*
1 *clove garlic*
1 *large avocado*

1 *tablespoon lemon juice*
Pinch of chilli powder
Salt and pepper

Peel the tomato and remove the seeds. Place the flesh in a blender goblet with the onion and garlic and liquidise until smooth. Peel and stone the avocado, add the flesh to the liquidiser with the lemon juice, chilli powder and a little salt and pepper. Switch on again until the mixture is smooth. Taste and adjust the seasoning if necessary. Pile up in a small bowl and serve with potato crisps or American corn chips.
Serves 4.

Variation:
Guacamole Omelette – Make up this spicy Mexican dip and use it as a filling for four two-egg omelettes. Sprinkle the folded omelettes with grated Parmesan cheese before serving.

HOT HERBED BREAD

1 long French loaf   *100 g (4 oz) herbed
                                        butter**

Have the herbed butter at room temperature. Cut the loaf diagonally into 2-cm ($\frac{3}{4}$ inch) slices and spread them generously with the herbed butter. Put the slices together to re-shape the loaf and wrap in foil. Place in a moderate oven (180°C, 350°F, Gas Mark 4) for 20 minutes.
Serves 4–6.
Variation:
Hot Lemon Garlic Bread – Combine 50 g (2 oz) each garlic butter* and lemon butter* and use to spread the bread slices.

VANILLA POURING SAUCE

300 ml ($\frac{1}{2}$ pint) milk   *$\frac{1}{2}$ teaspoon vanilla essence*
1 tablespoon cornflour   *15 g ($\frac{1}{2}$ oz) butter or*
2 tablespoons sugar   *margarine*

Put the milk, cornflour and sugar in a small pan and whisk over moderate heat until the sauce boils and thickens. Simmer for 2 minutes, stirring constantly, then beat in the vanilla essence and the butter.
Makes about 300 ml ($\frac{1}{2}$ pint).
Variations:
Mocha Sauce – Add 1 tablespoon cocoa and 1 teaspoon instant coffee powder with the cornflour and simmer the sauce for an extra 2 minutes. Omit the vanilla essence.
Brandy Sauce – Add 1–2 tablespoons brandy after the sauce is cooked and omit the vanilla essence.

BUTTERSCOTCH FUDGE SAUCE

100 g (4 oz) soft brown
  sugar
100 g (4 oz) golden syrup

25 g (1 oz) butter
2 tablespoons hot water
4 tablespoons single cream

Put the sugar, syrup and butter into a pan and stir over low heat until the sugar has dissolved. Boil for 3 minutes. Take off the heat and stir in the hot water very carefully as it will splutter. Cool for 3 minutes then stir in the cream. Serve hot.
Makes about 200 ml (6 fl oz).

CARAMEL SAUCE

50 g (2 oz) unsalted
  butter
6 tablespoons single
  cream

175 g (6 oz) demerara
  sugar

Place all the ingredients in a small pan and stir over moderate heat until the sugar has dissolved and the sauce is smooth and creamy. Serve hot or cold.
Makes about 200 ml (6 fl oz).

RICH CHOCOLATE SAUCE

175 g (6 oz) plain
  chocolate

15 g ($\frac{1}{2}$ oz) butter
4 tablespoons milk

Break up the chocolate and place in a basin over a pan of hot water. Add the butter and milk and stir until the ingredients blend together and the sauce is smooth.
Makes about 150 ml ($\frac{1}{4}$ pint).

ALL-PURPOSE BOLOGNESE SAUCE

50 g (2 oz) bacon, derinded
1 medium onion, chopped

1 teaspoon sugar
$\frac{1}{2}$ teaspoon dried basil

1 medium carrot, grated	$\frac{1}{4}$ teaspoon ground nutmeg
1 stick celery, chopped	150 ml ($\frac{1}{4}$ pint) dry white or
2 tablespoons oil	red wine
450 g (1 lb) minced beef	300 ml ($\frac{1}{2}$ pint) beef stock
2 tablespoons tomato purée	Salt and pepper

Chop the bacon and place in a large saucepan with the onion, carrot, celery and oil. Fry gently until the onion is soft but not brown. Add the beef and stir over moderate heat until it looks brown and crumbly. Add the tomato purée, sugar, basil, nutmeg, wine and stock and bring to the boil, stirring. Cook gently for about 40 minutes, or until the liquid has reduced and the meat sauce is thick. Add salt and pepper to taste and serve with freshly boiled pasta and grated Parmesan cheese.

Serves 4.

Variations:

High Speed Meat Sauce – Fry the onion in the oil and when soft add the meat and fry, stirring, until it looks brown and crumbly. Sprinkle in the contents of a 900 ml ($1\frac{1}{2}$ pint) packet of tomato soup mix and $\frac{1}{2}$ teaspoon dried mixed herbs. Stir well, add 450 ml ($\frac{3}{4}$ pint) water and bring to the boil, stirring constantly. Cook gently for 20 minutes and season to taste. Omit all other ingredients from the recipe.

Beefy Soup – Omit the bacon and wine. Use only 100 g (4 oz) minced beef and increase the beef stock to 1 litre ($1\frac{3}{4}$ pints). Cover and simmer for 30 minutes then moisten 1 tablespoon cornflour with a little cold water, add to the pan and bring back to the boil, stirring constantly. Simmer for a further 4 minutes and season to taste.

WHISKED BASIC WHITE SAUCE

25 g (1 oz) butter or	300 ml ($\frac{1}{2}$ pint) milk
margarine	Salt and pepper
25 g (1 oz) flour	

Place the butter, flour and milk in a saucepan and whisk over moderate heat until the sauce boils and thickens. Simmer for 2 minutes and season to taste.

Makes about 300 ml ($\frac{1}{2}$ pint).

Variations:

Cheese Sauce – Beat $\frac{1}{2}$ teaspoon dry mustard into the sauce then stir in 50 g (2 oz) grated Cheddar cheese until the sauce is again smooth. Check the seasoning before serving.

Onion Sauce – Chop 1 medium onion and fry gently in the butter until soft. Add the flour and milk and whisk until boiling, as above. Season with a pinch of ground nutmeg and salt and pepper to taste.

Parsley Sauce – Stir 4 tablespoons chopped parsley into the hot sauce and season well with salt and black pepper.

Egg Sauce – Chop 2 hard-boiled eggs and fold into the hot sauce. Season generously with salt and pepper and add 1–2 tablespoons single cream or evaporated milk.

BARBECUE BASTING SAUCE

1 large onion	2 tablespoons wine
2 cloves garlic	vinegar
4 tablespoons oil	1 teaspoon Tabasco
4 teaspoons cornflour	pepper sauce
300 ml ($\frac{1}{2}$ pint) water	100 g (4 oz) soft brown
2 tablespoons tomato	sugar
purée	Salt

Finely chop the onion and the garlic. Heat the oil in a pan and use to fry the onion and garlic gently until soft. Moisten the cornflour with a little of the water and add to the pan with the tomato purée, vinegar, Tabasco and sugar. Stir over the heat until well blended then gradually add the rest of the water and bring to the boil, stirring constantly. Simmer for 5 minutes and add salt to taste. This sauce is suitable for basting food during cooking or to serve with cooked food.

Makes about 450 ml ($\frac{3}{4}$ pint).

FRENCH DRESSING

2 tablespoons wine vinegar   6 tablespoons oil
1 teaspoon salt   Good pinch of sugar
1 teaspoon freshly
   ground black pepper

Place all the ingredients in a screw-topped jar and shake vigorously until the dressing thickens. Store in an airtight container in the refrigerator and shake well before each use.
Makes about 150 ml ($\frac{1}{4}$ pint).
Variations:
Garlic Dressing – Cut a clove of garlic in half and add the pieces to the dressing in the container. Discard when the container is empty.
Sauce Vinaigrette – Add 2 tablespoons finely chopped mixed herbs (such as parsley, marjoram, oregano, basil, or thyme) when making the dressing.

BLENDER MAYONNAISE

1 large egg   1 teaspoon sugar
$\frac{3}{4}$ teaspoon salt   1 tablespoon vinegar
$\frac{1}{2}$ teaspoon pepper   about 300 ml ($\frac{1}{2}$ pint) oil
$\frac{3}{4}$ teaspoon dry mustard

All the ingredients should be at room temperature. Place the egg in the blender goblet with the salt, pepper, mustard, sugar and vinegar. Switch on 'high' and leave for 15 seconds to mix. Start adding the oil, allowing it to trickle in slowly. When the mayonnaise starts to thicken, the oil can be added more quickly. If the mayonnaise becomes over-thick, add 1 tablespoon hot water and blend this in. Turn into an airtight container and store in the refrigerator. If by any chance the mayonnaise should curdle, tip it into a jug, place an egg yolk in the blender goblet and switch on 'high', adding the curdled mixture a little at a time until the mayonnaise emulsifies.
Makes about 300 ml ($\frac{1}{2}$ pint).

Variation:
Green mayonnaise – Very finely chop herbs such as parsley, chervil and chives to give 2 tablespoons. Stir into 150 ml ($\frac{1}{4}$ pint) mayonnaise and leave to stand for 10 minutes before serving.

SAVOURY BUTTERS

Cream *50 g (2 oz) butter* until really soft then gradually work in the chosen flavourings:
Curry Butter – 1 teaspoon lemon juice, 1 teaspoon curry powder and $\frac{1}{4}$ teaspoon ground turmeric.
Lemon Butter – 1 teaspoon lemon juice and 1 teaspoon finely grated lemon rind.
Herbed Butter – 1 teaspoon lemon juice and 1 teaspoon each chopped tarragon, chopped parsley and chopped chives.
Maitre d'Hotel Butter – 1 teaspoon lemon juice, 2 teaspoons very finely chopped parsley and a pinch of ground black pepper.
Mustard Butter – 2 teaspoons French mustard.
Garlic Butter – 1 clove garlic, very finely chopped.
When the butter has been combined with the flavouring, chill until firm enough to hold its shape then turn out on to a sheet of foil and form into a roll about 2.5 cm (1 inch) in diameter. Chill until required to serve. Cut into slices and place on hot fried or grilled meat or fish at serving time.
Serves 4.

Starters and Salads

TIPSY GRAPEFRUIT

2 grapefruit
2 tablespoons rum

2 tablespoons demerara
  sugar
½ teaspoon ground ginger

Halve the grapefruit and cut a sliver of skin from the base of each half so that it stands firmly. Loosen the segments and sprinkle the cut surfaces with the rum. Combine the sugar and ginger, sprinkle evenly over the tops and stand the grapefruit halves on a grid in the grill pan. Put under a hot grill until the sugar melts.
Serves 4.
Variation:
Ruby Beauties – Use pink grapefruit, substitute port for the rum, ground cinnamon for the ground ginger, and castor sugar for the demerara sugar.

ARTICHOKE AND MUSHROOM STARTER

396 g (14 oz) can artichoke
  hearts, drained
½ small sweet red pepper,
  deseeded

225 g (8 oz) button
  mushrooms, sliced
3 tablespoons French
  dressing
4 lettuce leaf 'cups'

If the artichoke hearts are rather large, halve them. Dice the pepper and place in a dish with the artichoke hearts and mushrooms. Sprinkle over the French dressing and toss lightly. Cover and leave to marinate for 1 hour. Serve in the lettuce leaf 'cups'.
Serves 4.

CREAMY PEAR STARTERS

lettuce leaves
2 tablespoons single
cream
4 tablespoons mayonnaise

2 large ripe but firm
Comice or Bartlett
pears
100 g (4 oz) cream cheese
with pineapple

Arrange lettuce leaves on 4 small side plates. Beat the cream into the mayonnaise. Peel the pears, halve them and scoop out the cores with a teaspoon, leaving neat hollows. Divide the cream cheese with pineapple into 4 equal portions and press one portion into each hollow in a pear half. Place one filled pear half, rounded side upwards, on each prepared plate and carefully spoon over the dressing to mask them completely.
Serves 4.

STRAWBERRY AND CUCUMBER SALAD

22.5 cm (9 inch) length
cucumber
Salt
225 g (8 oz) medium-
sized strawberries

4 tablespoons green
mayonnaise*
Snipped mustard and
cress

Peel and thinly slice the cucumber. Arrange the slices in a colander, sprinkle with salt and allow to stand for about 30 minutes. Drain well and dry on absorbent kitchen paper. Slice the strawberries and arrange with the cucumber slices in over-lapping circles on small side plates. Place a spoonful of mayonnaise in the centre of each plate and scatter mustard and cress over the top.
Serves 4.

AVOCADO MOUSSE

6 tablespoons white wine
15 g ($\frac{1}{2}$ oz) gelatine

Finely grated rind of
$\frac{1}{2}$ lemon

2 ripe avocados
150 ml ($\frac{1}{4}$ pint)
  mayonnaise*

Salt and pepper
150 ml ($\frac{1}{4}$ pint)
  whipping cream

Place the wine in a basin and sprinkle on the gelatine. Stand the
basin in a pan of hot water until the gelatine has completely dissolved. Halve, stone and peel the avocados and liquidise or beat
the flesh with the dissolved gelatine, mayonnaise and lemon
rind until smooth. Turn it into a bowl and season to taste with
salt and pepper. Whip the cream and when the avocado mixture
is on the point of setting, fold it in lightly. (If preferred, add a
drop or two of green food colouring to enhance the pale green
shade.) Divide between 4 individual dishes and allow to set.
Serves 4.

MUSHROOMS À LA GRECQUE

1 small onion
4 tablespoons olive oil
450 g (1 lb) button
  mushrooms
1 tablespoon tomato
  purée
4 tablespoons white wine

3 tablespoons lemon juice
1 bay leaf
$\frac{1}{2}$ teaspoon ground
  coriander
Salt and ground black
  pepper

Finely chop the onion and cook in the oil in a saucepan until
limp. Add the mushrooms and sauté until they are coated in the
oil mixture. Combine the tomato purée, wine and lemon juice
and add to the pan with the bay leaf, coriander and a little
seasoning. Bring to the boil then cover and simmer for 8
minutes, or until the mushrooms are just tender. Remove the
mushrooms to a serving dish with a slotted draining spoon and
discard the bay leaf. Boil the cooking liquid until it is reduced by
about one third, adjust the seasoning if necessary and pour it
over the mushrooms. Allow to cool then chill well before
serving.
Serves 4.

CUCUMBER AND LEMON CREAM STARTERS

½ cucumber
Salt and pepper
150 ml (¼ pint) double
  cream

Finely grated rind of 1
  lemon
Shredded lettuce
8 stuffed green olives, sliced

Peel and thinly slice the cucumber. Arrange the slices in a colander, sprinkle with salt and allow to stand for about 30 minutes. Drain well and dry on absorbent kitchen paper. Whip the cream with the lemon rind and season to taste with salt and pepper. Arrange a bed of shredded lettuce on each of 4 small side plates. Divide the cucumber slices between the plates, top each with a spoonful of the lemon cream and scatter over the olives.
Serves 4.

SARDINE-STUFFED ORANGES

2 large oranges
113 g (4 oz) can sardines
  in oil
100 g (4 oz) cream cheese
½ teaspoon French mustard
1 teaspoon grated onion
¼ teaspoon salt
½ teaspoon sweet paprika
  pepper

2 tablespoons soured
  cream
Freshly ground black
  pepper
4 lettuce leaves
2 tablespoons chopped
  parsley

Halve the oranges and carefully remove and reserve the pulp. Cut a sliver of rind from the base of each orange 'shell' so that it will stand firmly. Drain the sardines and mash with the cream cheese, mustard, onion, salt and paprika. Chop the orange flesh and fold into the fish mixture with the soured cream. Add a little of the orange juice but do not let the mixture become too wet. Season generously with pepper to taste and divide the mixture between the orange halves. Place each on a lettuce leaf on a small plate and sprinkle with parsley.
Serves 4.

CREAMY CHICKEN LIVER PÂTÉ

75 g (3 oz) butter
1 large onion, chopped
¼ teaspoon ground bay
   leaves
225 g (8 oz) chicken
   livers

1 tablespoon dry sherry
4 tablespoons single
   cream
Salt and black pepper

Melt one third of the butter and use to cook the onion with the
ground bay leaves until soft but not coloured. Add the livers and
cook gently for about 5 minutes, turning them occasionally,
until cooked through but just pink in the centre. Liquidise the
contents of the pan with the sherry, remaining butter and the
cream until the mixture is smooth. Season carefully with salt
and pepper and turn into a serving dish. Smooth the top, cover
and chill for 2 hours before serving.
Serves 4.

MACKEREL AND EGG PÂTÉ

225 g (8 oz) smoked
   mackerel fillet
50 g (2 oz) butter,
   softened
50 g (2 oz) cream cheese
½ teaspoon French
   mustard
2 tablespoons lemon juice

3 tablespoons single
   cream
Salt and pepper
1 hard-boiled egg,
   mashed
4 small lemon wedges
4 sprigs of parsley

Remove any skin from the mackerel and place in a blender with
the butter, cream cheese, mustard, lemon juice and cream.
Switch on until smooth or simply mash all the ingredients until
well combined. Taste and add salt and pepper if desired and stir
in the egg. Divide the pâté between 4 ramekin dishes and
garnish each with a lemon wedge and sprig of parsley. Serve
with toast fingers.
Serves 4.

LIVER AND BACON PÂTÉ

225 g (8 oz) lamb's liver
175 g (6 oz) pork
  sausagemeat
1 egg, beaten
1 tablespoon finely
  chopped parsley
3 tablespoons dry sherry

Pinch of ground cloves
$\frac{1}{2}$ teaspoon salt
$\frac{1}{4}$ teaspoon ground black
  pepper
175 g (6 oz) streaky
  bacon, derinded
1 bay leaf

Trim the liver and chop very finely, mince or liquidise until smooth. Place the sausagemeat in a bowl and gradually work in the egg, parsley, sherry, liver purée, cloves, salt and pepper. Use the bacon rashers to line a 450 g (1 lb) loaf tin and fill with the liver mixture. Fold over the ends of the bacon rashers if they protrude above the pâté. Put the bay leaf on top and cover lightly with a sheet of foil. Stand the tin in a roasting tin half filled with boiling water and cook in a moderately hot oven (190°C, 375°F, Gas Mark 5) for 1 hour. Remove from the oven, allow to cool and chill for 2 days to allow the pâté to mature before cutting. Serve with hot toast fingers.
Serves 4–6.

PIGS' LIVER PÂTÉ

175 g (6 oz) streaky
  bacon
2 medium onions, chopped
2 cloves garlic, crushed
450 g (1 lb) pigs' liver,
  sliced
$\frac{1}{4}$ teaspoon dried mixed
  herbs

1 tablespoon chopped
  sweet pepper
Salt and pepper
250 ml (9 fl oz) dry
  red wine
100 g (4 oz) butter,
  melted

Derind the bacon and place in an ovenproof basin with the onion, garlic, liver, herbs, sweet pepper and a little salt and pepper. Pour over the wine and press the ingredients so that they are under the liquid. Cover the basin with foil and smooth

down the edges. Stand in a saucepan and pour in boiling water to come half-way up the sides of the basin. Bring to the boil, cover the pan and keep the water bubbling gently for 3 hours, adding more boiling water when necessary. Drain off and reserve the cooking juices. Liquidise the liver mixture, adding sufficient of the reserved juices to make a firm paste. Add almost all the butter and liquidise again. Season to taste with more salt and pepper and turn into one large or two smaller serving dishes while still warm. Smooth the top and cover with the rest of the butter. Cool and chill until firm before serving.
Serves 8.

SILVERSIDE SALAD

1 large carrot	2 tablespoons chopped
4 large sticks celery	chives
225 g (8 oz) cooked	3 tablespoons sauce
silverside	vinaigrette*
	Shredded lettuce

Cut the carrot and celery into matchstick strips, removing any visible strings from the celery. Drop the strips into a pan of boiling salted water and cook for 4–5 minutes, until just tender but still firm. Drain well and allow to cool. Cut the meat into strips about the same size as the vegetables. Combine all the ingredients in a bowl and toss lightly. Serve on a bed of shredded lettuce.
Serves 4.
Variation:
Tongue Salad: Substitute canned lambs' tongues or ox tongue for the silverside, and a small head of fennel for the celery.

SLIMMERS' STUFFED TOMATOES

4 large tomatoes	198 g (7 oz) can tuna,
1 teaspoon grated onion	drained
100 g (4 oz) cottage	Salt and black pepper
cheese	Shredded lettuce

2 *tablespoons low calorie*
   salad dressing

Cut the top third off each tomato and reserve these 'lids'. Scoop out the centres of the tomatoes and mix with the onion, cottage cheese and salad dressing. Flake the tuna, fold in lightly and season with salt and black pepper. Cover and allow to stand for 20 minutes and at the same time, invert the tomato 'shells' so that they can drain. At serving time, fill the tomato cases with tuna filling, mounding tops, and place on a bed of lettuce on a serving dish. Set the lids on top at a slight angle, to show the filling.
Serves 4.

MINIATURE PASTA MOULDS

75 g (3 oz) short-cut
   macaroni
1 dessert apple, peeled
½ sweet green pepper,
   deseeded
1 teaspoon concentrated
   curry sauce

6 tablespoons mayonnaise*
75 g (3 oz) lean ham,
   diced
Lettuce leaves
Sprigs of parsley
Sprigs of watercress

Cook the macaroni in plenty of boiling salted water for about 12 minutes, or until tender but not too soft. Drain well. Meanwhile, core and chop the apple and finely dice the pepper. Beat together the curry sauce and mayonnaise and stir in the pasta, ham, apple and pepper. Divide the mixture between 6 small oiled dariole moulds or coffee cups and press down well with the back of a metal spoon. Chill for at least 2 hours. Arrange a bed of lettuce, parsley and watercress on a serving platter and unmould the pasta salads on this.
Serves 6.

MELON, CHICKEN AND POTATO SALAD

½ ripe honeydew melon
225 g (8 oz) cooked

Finely grated rind of 1
   orange

chicken, diced	150 ml ($\frac{1}{4}$ pint)
225 g (8 oz) cooked	mayonnaise*
potato, diced	Paprika pepper

Remove the melon flesh from the rind and cut it into neat dice. Place in a bowl with the chicken and potato. Beat the orange rind into the mayonnaise, spoon over the chicken mixture and toss lightly until coated. Chill for 30 minutes and serve in a salad bowl, sprinkled with paprika pepper.
Serves 4.

BROAD BEAN AND BACON SALAD

1 teaspoon ground turmeric	1 kg (2 lb) broad beans, shelled
1 tablespoon oil	2 tablespoons chopped parsley
3 tablespoons French dressing*	4 rashers streaky bacon, derinded
50 g (2 oz) long grain rice	

Beat the turmeric and oil into the French dressing and allow to stand at room temperature for 30 minutes. Cook the rice until tender, drain if necessary and fork up until fluffy. Pour over the dressing while the rice is still hot. Leave to cool. Meanwhile, cook the beans in a pan of boiling salted water for about 10 minutes, or until just tender. Drain well. When cold, fold into the rice mixture with the parsley. Grill the bacon until really crisp, drain on absorbent kitchen paper and crumble finely. Sprinkle the bacon bits over the salad. Serve with cold roast chicken or cooked fish.
Serves 4.

FRANKFURTERS WITH POTATO SALAD

450 g (1 lb) potatoes, diced	2 tablespoons chopped parsley

150 ml ($\frac{1}{4}$ pint) hot
  strong chicken stock
$\frac{1}{2}$ small onion, grated

150 ml ($\frac{1}{4}$ pint)
  mayonnaise*
8 frankfurter sausages
8 gherkins, sliced

Cook the potato in boiling salted water just to cover for about 5 minutes, or until tender but not broken. Drain well and immediately pour over the chicken stock. Stir in the onion, parsley and mayonnaise and leave to stand until cold. At serving time, place the sausages in a pan of water, bring to boiling point, cover the pan and allow to stand for 5 minutes. Drain well. Pile up the potato salad on a serving platter and arrange the hot sausages on top. Sprinkle over the gherkin.
Serves 4.

GARLIC SAUSAGE AND FRENCH BEAN SALAD

350 g (12 oz) French beans
450 ml ($\frac{3}{4}$ pint) chicken
  stock
1 egg, hard-boiled
$\frac{1}{2}$ medium cucumber,
  sliced

100 g (4 oz) garlic
  sausage
3 tablespoons sauce
  vinaigrette*
4 spring onions, chopped

Top and tail the beans and halve any large ones. Cook in the chicken stock for about 4 minutes, or until just beginning to soften. Drain and cool. Halve the egg, remove the yolk and finely chop the white. Arrange the cucumber slices round the edge of a serving platter. Cut the garlic sausage into thin strips and mix with the beans and egg white. Combine the sauce vinaigrette and spring onion, pour over the bean mixture, toss lightly and pile into the centre of the dish. Press the egg yolk through a sieve over the top of the salad.
Serves 4.

GERMAN POTATO SALAD

0.5 kg (1 $\frac{1}{4}$ lb) medium
  potatoes

5 tablespoons cider
  vinegar

6 rashers streaky bacon,
  derinded
1 small onion, chopped
1 tablespoon flour

150 ml ($\frac{1}{4}$ pint) water
1 tablespoon sugar
1 teaspoon salt
Black pepper

It is important that the potatoes are all of an even size so that
they cook in the same length of time. Scrub the potatoes and
cook in boiling salted water for about 20 minutes, or until tender
but not soft. Drain and when the potatoes are cool enough to
handle, peel them and cut into cubes. Chop the bacon and fry
gently in a large pan until the fat runs freely and the bacon bits
are golden and crisp. Remove them with a slotted draining
spoon and add the onion to the fat in the pan. Fry gently until
golden then stir in the flour. When well blended gradually add
the vinegar and water and bring to the boil, stirring constantly,
until the mixture thickens. Mix in the sugar and add salt and
pepper to taste. Fold in the potato and bacon bits and cook
gently, stirring occasionally, for 5 minutes, or until piping hot.
Serves 4.

JELLIED TOMATO RING

25 g (1 oz) butter
50 g (2 oz) button
  mushrooms, sliced
1 small onion, chopped
600 ml (1 pint) tomato
  juice
$\frac{1}{4}$ teaspoon ground allspice
Pinch of dried marjoram
1 teaspoon sugar

Few drops Tabasco pepper
  sauce
Salt
20 g ($\frac{3}{4}$ oz) gelatine
2 tablespoons water
150 ml ($\frac{1}{4}$ pint) evaporated
  milk
1 tablespoon lemon juice
Shredded lettuce

Melt the butter and use to fry the mushroom and onion gently
until the onion is soft. Pour in the tomato juice, add the allspice,
marjoram, sugar and Tabasco and bring to the boil. Cook gently
for 10 minutes. Liquidise the mixture or press it through a sieve
and add salt to taste. Dissolve the gelatine in the water in a basin
over a pan of hot water. Blend into the tomato liquid and allow

to cool. Place the evaporated milk and lemon juice in a bowl and whisk steadily until thick. Gradually add the tomato mixture, whisking all the time, until well combined and fluffy. Pour into an oiled 1 litre (1¾ pint) ring mould and chill until set. Turn out on a bed of shredded lettuce to serve.
Serves 4.

MINTED BEAN SALAD

100 g (4 oz) dried haricot beans	½ teaspoon concentrated mint sauce
100 g (4 oz) dried red kidney beans	2 teaspoons salt
750 ml (1¼ pints) chicken stock	2 teaspoons sugar
	4 tablespoons olive oil
100 g (4 oz) black olives	4 tablespoons lemon juice
2 large tomatoes	Pepper

Soak the beans together in cold water to cover overnight. Drain well, pour over the stock and bring to the boil. Cover and simmer for about 1 hour, or until the beans are tender but not mushy. Drain well. Halve and stone the olives and chop the tomatoes. Place these in a salad bowl with the beans. Mix together the mint sauce, salt, sugar, olive oil and lemon juice in a screw topped jar and shake well until blended. Pour over the bean salad and toss lightly. Add pepper to taste, cover and chill before serving.
Serves 4.
Variation:
Easy Bean Salad – Drain a 425 g (15 oz) can of cannellini beans and use to make the salad. Substitute 75 g (3 oz) stuffed green olives for the black olives.

CHINESE LEAF AND PINEAPPLE SALAD

225 g (8 oz) can pineapple pieces	50 g (2 oz) small pasta shapes, cooked

1 tablespoon peanut
    butter
1 tablespoon French
    dressing

8 leaves from a head of
    Chinese leaves

Drain the pineapple and combine the syrup with the peanut butter and French dressing. Stir in the pineapple pieces and pasta and chill for 30 minutes. Remove the thick rib from the base of each Chinese leaf and shred the remainder. Fold into the pineapple mixture just before serving.
Serves 4.

SPINACH AND BEETROOT SALAD

100 g (4 oz) fresh spinach
100 g (4 oz) bean sprouts
8 small sprigs
    watercress
1 tablespoon French
    dressing

3 tablespoons orange
    juice
Finely grated rind of
    1 small orange
150 ml ($\frac{1}{4}$ pint) natural
    yogurt
1 quantity garlic chapons*

Trim the spinach leaves, remove the stalks and tear up the leaves. Place in a salad bowl with the bean sprouts and watercress. Beat the French dressing, orange juice and rind into the yogurt and pour over the salad ingredients. Toss lightly until coated, sprinkle with the chapons and serve immediately. This salad is excellent with cold roast pork or beef.
Serves 4.

DRESS-UPS FOR COLESLAW

It is hardly worth making your own coleslaw as it is so easy to buy ready-made. However, bought coleslaw is easily recognisable and it can be quite transformed in any of these simple ways. Quantities are planned to combine with a 225 g (8 oz) carton of coleslaw.

Curly Cabbage Coleslaw – Cut off the top third of a medium sized savoy cabbage and trim the base so it will stand firmly. Using a sharp pointed knife, cut out the centre from the base leaving a cabbage 'bowl' to hold the coleslaw. Wash and drain well. Shred some of the cabbage heart and add to the bought coleslaw which will give a pleasant speckled green effect. Stir in extra mayonnaise if necessary. Serve piled up in the cabbage 'bowl'.

Apple Coleslaw – Remove the core from a large green-skinned dessert apple and slice it finely. Stir into the bought coleslaw with, if liked, a few chopped walnuts or peanuts.

Cheesy Coleslaw – Scrape and coarsely grate 1 large carrot. Stir into the coleslaw with 25 g (1 oz) sultanas and 50 g (2 oz) finely diced Gouda cheese.

IMPROVING BOUGHT SALAD DRESSINGS

Salad Cream: The flavour is quite strong and recognisable straight from the bottle, but as a basis for creamy-textured dressings it is a great time saver.

Seafood Sauce – Beat 1 tablespoon tomato ketchup into 4 tablespoons salad cream. Fold in 2 tablespoons finely chopped spring onion and 1 tablespoon finely chopped green pepper.

Soured Cream Sauce – Beat 4 tablespoons soured cream into an equal quantity of salad cream with 1 teaspoon grated onion. This sauce can be varied by adding finely chopped fresh green herbs to taste.

Mayonnaise: Those described as 'lemon' mayonnaise often taste very similar to a home-made one, but any good bought mayonnaise is satisfactory as the basis for either of the following dressings.

Green Goddess Dressing – Finely chop 2 anchovy fillets and beat into 6 tablespoons mayonnaise with 2 teaspoons white vinegar, a pinch of dried tarragon and 1 tablespoon each of chopped parsley and chives. To improve the colour, add 1 drop of green food colouring.

Thousand Island Dressing – Blend 6 tablespoons mayonnaise with 1 tablespoon mild chilli sauce, 1 tablespoon finely chopped sweet red pepper and 1 teaspoon grated onion.

Fish

PRAWN STROGANOFF

50 g (2 oz) butter
1 small onion, chopped
1 clove garlic, crushed
100 g (4 oz) button
   mushrooms, sliced
25 g (1 oz) flour
300 ml ($\frac{1}{2}$ pint) dry
   white wine

150 ml ($\frac{1}{4}$ pint) soured
   cream
4 tablespoons medium
   dry sherry
225 g (8 oz) peeled
   prawns
Salt and pepper

Melt the butter in a frying pan and use to fry the onion and garlic gently until soft but not brown. Add the mushrooms and cook for a further 2 minutes. Stir in the flour and when well blended, cook for 1 minute then gradually mix in the wine and bring to the boil, stirring. Simmer for 4 minutes, stir in the soured cream, sherry, prawns and seasoning to taste. Heat through thoroughly and serve with cooked rice or noodles, and a salad. Serves 4.

Variation:
For a more economical dish – Substitute dry cider for the white wine.

CRAB AU GRATIN

225 g (8 oz) crab meat,
   either white, dark, or
   a mixture of the two
1 egg, beaten
4 tablespoons double
   cream
1 tablespoon
   Worcestershire sauce

1 teaspoon curry powder
Salt and pepper
4 tablespoons fresh
   white breadcrumbs
25 g (1 oz) butter
100 g (4 oz) cheese, grated

Mix the crab meat with the egg, cream, Worcestershire sauce, curry powder and salt and pepper to taste. Divide between 4 greased deep scallop shells or small ovenproof dishes. Fry the breadcrumbs in the butter until pale golden, sprinkle over the crab mixture with the grated cheese. Place on a baking sheet and cook in a moderately hot oven (190°C, 375°F, Gas Mark 5) for 20–25 minutes. Serve piping hot, with a green salad.
Serves 4 as a starter, or 2 as a main course.

Variation:

Salmon au Gratin – Use flaked cooked or canned salmon instead of the crab and garnish with slices of cucumber and lemon.

CREAMY MOULES MARINIÈRE

2 litres (3 pints) mussels
1 large onion, chopped
2 cloves garlic, crushed
50 g (2 oz) butter
4 tablespoons olive oil

200 ml ($\frac{1}{3}$ pint) dry white wine or cider
150 ml ($\frac{1}{4}$ pint) double cream
4 tablespoons chopped parsley
Salt and pepper

It is very important that the mussels are scrupulously clean and in perfect condition before cooking. Discard any with broken shells, as this indicates that the fish inside are dead. Scrub the mussels thoroughly in cold water with a stiff brush. Any mussels that are not tightly closed should be thrown away. Fry the onion and garlic gently in the butter and oil in a deep saucepan for 2–3 minutes. Add the cleaned mussels and cook for 3 minutes, shaking the pan from time to time. Add the white wine and continue cooking until the mussel shells open – this will only take a few minutes. Discard any that do not open. Stir in the cream, parsley and salt and pepper to taste. Heat through until the sauce is piping hot, then serve immediately in soup bowls, with plenty of crusty bread.
Serves 4.

SALMON RING

15 g ($\frac{1}{2}$ oz) gelatine
2 tablespoons water
298 g (10$\frac{1}{2}$ oz) can
  condensed celery soup
225 g (8 oz) cottage
  cheese, sieved

200 g (7 oz) cooked salmon
  or salmon trout
2 tablespoons vinegar
2 tablespoons mayonnaise
Salt and pepper
Sprigs of watercress

Dissolve the gelatine in the water in a basin over a pan of hot water. Put the soup and cottage cheese in a bowl and mix well. Drain the salmon, remove any skin and the large central bones. Flake the fish roughly and add to the soup mixture with the vinegar and mayonnaise. When well combined, season to taste. Add the dissolved gelatine and mix thoroughly. Transfer to an oiled 900 ml (1$\frac{1}{2}$ pint) ring mould and chill until set. Turn out on a serving dish and garnish the mould with sprigs of watercress. Alternatively, divide the mixture between individual serving dishes and serve each with a sprig of watercress on top. Serves 4–6.

BAKED FISH WITH ORANGE

4 cutlets of white fish
  such as cod, halibut
  or turbot
50 g (2 oz) butter
4 spring onions, chopped
Salt and pepper

Grated rind and juice
  of 2 oranges
Peeled segments from
  2 oranges
Sprigs of parsley

Arrange the cutlets in a shallow ovenproof dish. Dot with the butter and scatter over the onion. Sprinkle with salt and pepper and pour over the orange rind and juice. Cover with a piece of foil, shiny side downwards, and bake in a moderately hot oven (190°C, 375°F, Gas Mark 5) for 25–30 minutes, until the fish flakes easily when tested with a fork. Remove the cutlets to a warm serving dish, spoon over the cooking juices and serve hot, garnished with the orange segments and parsley sprigs. Serves 4.

Fish with Orange Mayonnaise – Bake the fish as above, using only the orange juice and not the rind. Place the cooked fish on a serving dish, discarding any liquid. Mix 150 ml ($\frac{1}{4}$ pint) mayonnaise with 150 ml ($\frac{1}{4}$ pint) double cream and the grated rind from the 2 oranges. Spoon over the cool fish and chill for 2 hours. Garnish with orange segments and parsley.

PLAICE IN NUTTY BUTTER

8 small plaice fillets
2 tablespoons seasoned
  flour
100 g (4 oz) butter
2 tablespoons oil

40 g (1 $\frac{1}{2}$ oz) flaked
  almonds
2 tablespoons lemon
  juice
Salt and pepper

Coat the fish with seasoned flour. Heat half the butter in a large shallow pan with the oil. Put in the fish, if necessary in two batches, and fry gently for about 6 minutes, turning once. Transfer the fish to a serving dish and keep warm. Add the remaining butter to the fat in the pan and heat briskly until it turns golden brown. Sprinkle in the almonds and as soon as they are lightly browned, stir in the lemon juice. Season to taste and pour over the fish. Serve hot.
Serves 4.
Variation:
Plaice in Tarragon Butter – Cook the fish as above and keep warm. When the remaining butter is added to the pan, allow it to melt but not brown. Add 2 tablespoons chopped tarragon and 2 tablespoons lemon juice. When the butter is really hot spoon it over the fish and serve immediately.

SMOKED FISH BALLS

450 g (1 lb) smoked cod
  or haddock fillet
1 bay leaf

2 eggs, beaten
Flour for coating
100 g (4 oz) fresh white

Salt and pepper
225 g (8 oz) potatoes
50 g (2 oz) butter or
  margarine
1 small onion, chopped

breadcrumbs
Oil for deep frying
Lemon wedges
Mayonnaise

Put the smoked fish into a shallow pan with the bay leaf and a little pepper. Add sufficient water just to cover the fish. Put on the lid and poach gently for 10–12 minutes, or until the fish flakes easily when tested with a fork. Drain the fish, discard any skin and bones, and flake roughly. Cook the potatoes in boiling salted water until tender. Drain well and mash with half the butter. Melt the remaining butter in a pan and use to fry the onion until soft. Add the fish, mashed potato and half the beaten egg and season with salt and pepper to taste. Chill for 30 minutes. Shape the mixture into small balls, each about the size of a walnut. Coat them in flour, dip in the rest of the beaten egg and cover evenly with breadcrumbs. Deep fry the fish balls, in batches, in hot oil, for 3–4 minutes, or until crisp and golden. Drain well on absorbent paper and serve hot, piled up on a serving dish, garnished with lemon wedges. Hand a bowl of mayonnaise separately.
Serves 4.

FISH GOUJONS

0.75 kg (1 $\frac{1}{2}$ lb) white
  fish fillets, such as
  lemon sole
Seasoned flour
Beaten egg
Dried breadcrumbs
4 tablespoons mayonnaise
4 tablespoons soured
  cream

6 gherkins, chopped
2 tablespoons drained
  capers
2 tablespoons chopped
  parsley
Salt and pepper
Oil for deep frying
Lemon wedges

Cut the fish into small strips, each about 7.5 cm (3 inches) by 1.25 cm ($\frac{1}{2}$ inch) and coat them in seasoned flour. Dip in beaten egg and cover evenly in breadcrumbs. Chill for 1 hour. Meanwhile, make the sauce. Mix the mayonnaise with the soured cream, gherkins, capers, parsley and salt and pepper to taste. Deep fry the fish strips, in batches, in hot oil for about 2–3 minutes, until crisp and golden. Drain well on absorbent paper. Serve hot, piled up on a serving dish and garnished with lemon wedges. Hand the sauce separately.

Serves 4.

FISH BURGERS

350 g (12 oz) white fish fillets	1 teaspoon dried mixed herbs
300 ml (½ pint) milk	3 tablespoons chopped parsley
1 bay leaf	
Salt and pepper	1 egg, beaten
1 small onion, grated	Oil for shallow frying
75 g (3 oz) fresh white breadcrumbs	1 tablespoon cornflour
	Anchovy essence
Grated rind and juice of ½ lemon	

Put the fish in a shallow pan with the milk, bay leaf and a little salt and pepper. Cover and poach for about 10 minutes, until the fish flakes easily when tested with a fork. Drain off and reserve the cooking liquid. Flake the fish, discarding any skin and bones, and mix with the onion, breadcrumbs, lemon rind and juice, mixed herbs, parsley, egg and salt and pepper to taste. Divide into 4 equal portions and shape each into a round, flat cake. Shallow fry in hot oil for about 3 minutes on each side, until golden brown. Drain well on absorbent paper. Meanwhile, make up the cooking liquid to 400 ml (14 fl oz) with water and bring to the boil. Moisten the cornflour with a little cold water, add to the pan and stir over the heat until the sauce boils and thickens. Simmer for 2 minutes and add anchovy essence to taste. Serve hot with the burgers.

Serves 4.

FISH STEAKS WITH BUTTER BEANS

1 green pepper, deseeded
25 g (1 oz) butter
1 tablespoon oil
1 medium onion, chopped
425 g (15 oz) can butter
  beans, drained

4 frozen fish steaks,
  defrosted
Salt and pepper
75 g (3 oz) Cheddar
  cheese, grated

Chop the pepper and fry in the butter and oil with the onion until soft. Stir in the butter beans and transfer this mixture to a shallow ovenproof dish. Arrange the fish steaks on top and sprinkle with salt and pepper. Scatter over the cheese, cover and cook in a moderate oven (180°C, 350°F, Gas Mark 4) for 25 minutes. Remove the cover and return to the oven for a further 10 minutes, or until the top is golden brown.

Serves 4.

Variation:

Fish Steaks with Sweetcorn – Substitute a drained 325 g (11 $\frac{1}{2}$ oz) can of sweetcorn kernels for the butter beans and season the fish steaks with garlic salt and pepper.

MACKEREL WITH BACON

100 g (4 oz) herbed
  butter*
4 medium mackerel,
  cleaned

Salt and pepper
4 large rashers bacon,
  derinded

Divide the butter into 8 equal portions. Sprinkle inside each mackerel with salt and pepper, put in a portion of butter and reshape the fish. Have ready 4 large rectangles of well-greased foil, each large enough to enclose a fish completely. Wrap a rasher of bacon around each mackerel, place on a piece of foil and bring up the edges, crimping them to make airtight parcels. Place on a baking sheet or in a roasting tin and cook in a hot oven (220°C, 425°F, Gas Mark 7) for 30 minutes. Open the parcels, top each fish with a portion of the remaining butter and serve with boiled potatoes.

Serves 4.

HERRING SALAD

4 mateus herring fillets,
  drained
1 dessert apple, cored
225 g (8 oz) cooked new
  potatoes
1 small cooked beetroot
  sliced

150 ml ($\frac{1}{4}$ pint) soured
  cream
2 tablespoons chopped
  mixed fresh herbs
Salt and pepper
Lettuce leaves
Few onion rings

Cut the herring fillets into chunks and dice the apple and
potatoes. Combine the fish, beetroot, apple, potato, soured
cream and herbs and season lightly to taste. Serve on lettuce
leaves garnished with onion rings.
Serves 4.

SWEET SOUR GRILLED HERRINGS

4 medium herrings,
  cleaned
Oil
Salt and pepper
1 tablespoon French
  mustard

2 tablespoons wine vinegar
2 tablespoons demerara
  sugar
Finely grated rind
  of 1 orange
Sprigs of watercress

Have the herrings scaled and cleaned by the fishmonger. Slash
them diagonally in 3 places through the thick part of each fish,
brush with oil and sprinkle with salt and pepper. Place the fish
on a rack in the grill pan and cook under a hot grill for 4 minutes.
Meanwhile, mix together the mustard, wine vinegar, sugar and
orange rind. Turn the herrings carefully. Brush with a little
more oil and spoon over the mustard mixture. Grill for a further
4 minutes, or until the fish are cooked. Serve hot garnished with
watercress.
Serves 4.
Variation:
Normandy Herrings – Put a tablespoon of raisins into the
cavity of each cleaned fish. Brush with oil, sprinkle with salt and

pepper and grill for 4 minutes as above. Turn the fish, and brush with 4 tablespoons melted crab apple or gooseberry jelly instead of the mustard mixture. Grill for a further 4 minutes, or until cooked.

CÉVICHE (MARINATED RAW FISH)

6 *plaice fillets*	*Salt and pepper*
8 *limes or 6 lemons*	*Lettuce leaves*
2 *large onions*	2 *tablespoons chopped*
2 *cloves garlic, crushed*	*mint*
$\frac{1}{4}$ *teaspoon hot chilli powder*	

The fish used in this recipe must be very fresh, as it is not actually cooked. Skin the fish and cut each fillet into 4 or 6 even-sized pieces. Place in a shallow dish and squeeze over the juice from the limes or lemons. Thinly slice the onions and divide into rings. Add to the dish with the garlic and chilli powder. Sprinkle with salt and pepper and mix all the ingredients lightly together. Cover and chill for at least 4 hours, or until the fish has become opaque and white, turning the fish pieces 2 or 3 times during chilling. Arrange the marinated fish on a bed of lettuce on a serving dish, top with the onion rings and spoon over the citrus juices. Sprinkle with chopped mint and serve with plain boiled potatoes.
Serves 4.

Meat and Poultry

This section covers what is usually the most expensive part of the menu and involves a number of cooking techniques. Roasting is quite rightly considered the most difficult because the temperature and time chosen for cooking joints and whole birds are so important. The other most used methods of cooking are braising, stewing, frying and grilling. Recipes are given to illustrate all these methods and a useful roasting chart is included.

TRADITIONAL ROAST BEEF DINNER

1.5 kg (3 lb) joint topside of beef	*YORKSHIRE PUDDING BATTER:*
75 g (3 oz) beef dripping or 5 tablespoons oil	100 g (4 oz) plain flour $\frac{1}{2}$ teaspoon salt
1 kg (2 lb) potatoes	1 egg
Salt	300 ml ($\frac{1}{2}$ pint) milk
Gravy mix	50 g (2 oz) lard

Put the joint in a roasting tin with the dripping or oil and place in a hot oven (220°C, 425°F, Gas Mark 7) for 20 minutes. Meanwhile, cut the potatoes into even-sized pieces and cook in boiling salted water to cover for 3 minutes. Drain well and shake the potatoes in the pan. Arrange the potatoes round the joint and baste with the hot fat. Sprinkle with salt and return the roasting tin to the oven for a further 1 hour. While the joint is in the oven, prepare the batter for the Yorkshire pudding. Sift the flour and salt into a bowl, make a well in the centre and add the egg and half the milk. Beat with a wooden spoon, gradually drawing in the dry ingredients, until the batter is smooth, then work in the rest of the milk. Leave the batter to stand. Thirty minutes before the meat will be ready, put the lard in another roasting tin or baking tin and place on a shelf in the oven above the meat. When the fat is hot enough to make the batter sizzle on contact, pour it in all at once and bake for 30 minutes, or until the pudding is risen and well browned. Remove the meat and potatoes from the oven while the pudding cooks for a further 5 minutes. Transfer the joint and potatoes to warm serving dishes, spoon off excess fat from the juices in the tin if desired, and make the gravy. Serve the meat sliced with roast potatoes and portions of Yorkshire pudding.

Serves 4, with extra meat to serve cold.

Note: To make thick gravy, either stir a little flour into the pan juices, then add water drained from cooking green vegetables and place over the heat, stirring constantly until the gravy becomes thick and smooth. Alternatively, add gravy powder mixed with cold water to the juices and then hot water from the vegetables to prevent lumps from forming.

Variation:

Individual Yorkshire Puddings — Put $\frac{1}{2}$ teaspoon oil into each of 8 deep bun tins and heat in the oven as above. Pour in the batter to fill the tins about two-thirds full and bake above the meat for 20–25 minutes.

BOILED SILVERSIDE WITH DUMPLINGS

1.5 kg (3 lb) joint salted silverside	4 small onions
8 peppercorns	DUMPLINGS:
3 cloves	225 g (8 oz) self-raising flour
1 teaspoon dried mixed herbs	$\frac{3}{4}$ teaspoon salt
8 small carrots	$\frac{1}{4}$ teaspoon pepper
	100 g (4 oz) shredded suet

Place the joint in a large saucepan and pour over water to cover. Bring to the boil and add the peppercorns, cloves, and herbs. Cover and simmer for $1\frac{3}{4}$ hours. Put in the carrots and onions, bring back to simmering point and cook for a further 15 minutes. Meanwhile, make the dumplings. Sift the flour, salt and pepper together and stir in the suet and sufficient cold water to make a fairly firm dough. Divide into 8 equal portions and shape each into a ball with floured hands. Add the dumplings to the stock in the pan, put on the lid and cook for 30 minutes, turning the dumplings once during this time. Transfer the joint to a hot serving dish and surround with the vegetables and dumplings. (Reserve the well-flavoured cooking stock to make soup.)

Serves 4, with extra meat to serve cold.

Note: Dumplings can be cooked separately in a pan of salted boiling water then drained and served with any meat stew.

Variation:

Parsley Dumplings − Add 2 tablespoons chopped parsley to the dry ingredients with the suet.

TAVERNER'S BEEF STEW WITH CROÛTONS

1 tablespoon oil
1 large onion, chopped
0.5 kg (1¼ lb) stewing
   steak, cubed
2 tablespoons flour
450 ml (¾ pint) light ale

50 g (2 oz) seedless
   raisins
1 beef stock cube
1 tablespoon French
   mustard
Salt and pepper
Mustard croûtons*

Heat the oil in a large pan and use to fry the onion and meat until the meat is sealed on all sides. Stir in the flour and when well blended add the ale and bring to the boil, stirring constantly. Sprinkle in the raisins, crumble in the stock cube and add the mustard and stir well. Cover and simmer for 1½ hours, or until the meat is tender. Season to taste with salt and pepper and serve garnished with the mustard croûtons.

Serves 4.

PEPPERED SIRLOIN STEAKS

4 *small sirloin steaks*
1 *tablespoon whole black*
  peppercorns
25 g (1 oz) *butter*
1 *tablespoon oil*

2 *tablespoons brandy*
150 ml ($\frac{1}{4}$ *pint*) *double*
  cream
Salt

Trim the steaks neatly. Crush the peppercorns fairly finely using a wooden board and rolling pin. Press the crushed peppercorns into both sides of the meat, taking care to make them adhere. Heat the butter and oil together in a frying pan and use to cook the steaks over high heat for 1 minute on each side to seal them. Reduce the heat and continue cooking for a further 2–5 minutes on each side according to whether you like your steaks rare or well done. Remove the steaks to a warm serving dish, add the brandy to the juices in the pan, ignite and remove from the heat. When the flames die down, gradually add the cream and stir thoroughly. Season to taste with salt and reheat carefully but do not allow the sauce to boil. Spoon over the steaks before serving.
Serves 4.
Note: Thin rump steaks can be used or even tenderised steaks for this dish.

MINCE SPECIALS

Minced beef is undoubtedly the most popular meat choice today. The following recipes can also be made with minced lamb or pork which are little more expensive but less readily available. The recipes are also ideal to prepare using part TVP (textured vegetable protein) made from soya beans. You can substitute half or even two thirds of the meat with TVP granules. But if you buy complete mixes which include all necessary ingredients with the granules, be sure to follow the pack instructions.

MINCE MOUSSAKA

2 tablespoons oil
1 medium onion, chopped
450 g (1 lb) minced beef
225 g (8 oz) can tomatoes
2 tablespoons tomato
   purée
$\frac{1}{2}$ teaspoon sugar
Salt and pepper

0.75 kg (1 $\frac{1}{2}$ lb) potatoes
Oil for deep frying
1 tablespoon cornflour
1 egg, separated
300 ml ($\frac{1}{2}$ pint) whisked
   cheese sauce*
40 g (1 $\frac{1}{2}$ oz) Cheddar
   cheese, grated

Heat the measured quantity of oil and use to fry the onion
gently. When it is soft, add the beef and stir over moderate heat
until it looks brown and crumbly. Drain the tomatoes, reserving
the liquid. Roughly chop the tomatoes and mix into the meat
with the tomato purée, sugar and a little seasoning. Bring to the
boil, stirring, then simmer for 30 minutes. Meanwhile, thinly
slice the potatoes and fry in hot oil until golden brown all over.
Drain well. Blend the cornflour with the reserved liquid, add to
the meat mixture and bring to the boil, stirring constantly.
Simmer for 2 minutes then check the seasoning. Put half the
meat mixture into an ovenproof dish, cover with half the potato
slices then repeat the layers. Beat the egg yolk into the cheese
sauce. Whisk the egg white until stiff and fold in gently. Spread
over the ingredients in the dish and sprinkle with the cheese.
Bake in a moderate oven (180°C, 350°F, Gas Mark 4) for about
30 minutes, or until golden brown on the top.
Serves 4–6.

FRUITED MINCED BEEF

2 tablespoons oil
1 medium onion, chopped
2 sticks celery, chopped
$\frac{1}{2}$ teaspoon curry powder
450 g (1 lb) minced beef
2 tablespoons flour
150 ml ($\frac{1}{4}$ pint) water

1 beef stock cube
50 g (2 oz) sultanas,
   raisins or chopped
   dried apricots
25 g (1 oz) toasted
   flaked almonds
Salt and pepper

Heat the oil and use to fry the onion, celery and curry powder gently until the onion is soft. Add the beef and stir over moderate heat until it looks brown and crumbly. Stir in the flour and when well blended add the water and bring to the boil, stirring constantly. Mix in the stock cube, dried fruit and almonds, cover and cook gently for 40 minutes, stirring occasionally. Season to taste with salt and pepper and serve with vegetables or fluffy boiled rice.

Serves 4.

BEEF STEW WITH PASTA

1 large onion, sliced
2 tablespoons oil
450 g (1 lb) minced beef
2 tablespoons flour
2 tablespoons tomato
  purée
1 beef stock cube,
  crumbled

2 teaspoons sweet
  paprika pepper
425 g (15 oz) can tomatoes
4 tablespoons water
100 g (4 oz) pasta shells
Salt and pepper

Fry the onion gently in the oil until soft. Add the beef and fry, stirring, until it looks brown and crumbly. Stir in the flour, tomato purée, stock cube and paprika and when well mixed in, put in the tomatoes and liquid from the can, the water and pasta shells. Bring to the boil, stirring. Cover and simmer for 40 minutes, stirring occasionally so that the mixture does not stick. Add salt and pepper to taste and serve hot with a green vegetable.

Serves 4.

MADRAS CURRY WITH SIDE DISHES

2 tablespoons oil
2 large onions, sliced
0.5 kg (1 ¼ lb) lean
  braising steak, cubed

ONION AND PEPPER
  SAMBAL:
1 small onion
½ small green pepper,

Salt

2 tablespoons curry
powder

Large pinch of ground
ginger

Large pinch of ground
cinnamon

Large pinch of ground
cloves

1 teaspoon brown sugar

2 beef stock cubes

Finely grated rind and
juice of 1 lemon

deseeded

Juice of 1 lime or
1 lemon

Salt and pepper

*MINTED YOGURT WITH
CUCUMBER:*

10 cm (4 inch) length
cucumber, diced

$\frac{1}{4}$ teaspoon concentrated
mint sauce

150 ml ($\frac{1}{4}$ pint) natural
yogurt

Heat the oil and use to fry the onion gently for 2 minutes.
Sprinkle the meat with salt, add to the pan and fry gently until
sealed on all sides. Sprinkle in the curry powder, ginger, cinnamon, cloves and sugar and stir-fry for 4 minutes. Crumble in the
stock cubes, add the lemon rind and juice and just sufficient
water to cover the meat. Stir well, bring to the boil then reduce
the heat and simmer for 2 hours, or until the meat is tender and
the liquid well reduced. Meanwhile, make the side dishes. For
the sambal, finely slice the onion and pepper and arrange in a
small dish. Sprinkle over the fruit juice and sprinkle lightly with
salt and pepper. Toss the ingredients well together before
serving. For the cucumber side dish, place the cucumber in a
shallow bowl. Beat the mint sauce into the yogurt and pour over
the cucumber. Stir lightly before serving. Check the curry and
add salt to taste. Serve with plenty of fluffy boiled rice and the
side dishes.
Serves 4.

ROAST LAMB WITH GARLIC AND ROSEMARY

1.75 kg (4 lb) joint leg
or shoulder of lamb

1 tablespoon oil

Salt and pepper

2–3 cloves garlic

2 teaspoons dried
rosemary

Slash the skin of the joint on the top surface in parallel lines about 2.5 cm (1 inch) apart in each direction to make diamond shapes. Insert the tip of a sharp pointed knife where the lines cross. Brush the skin with oil and sprinkle generously with salt and pepper. Cut each clove of garlic into 3 or 4 slivers, cut these in half across and insert the pointed ends into the cuts. Sprinkle over the rosemary and place in a roasting tin. Cook in moderate oven (180°C, 350°F, Gas Mark 4) for 35 minutes per 450 g (1 lb), basting with the pan juices about 30 minutes before the end of cooking time.

Serves 4, with extra meat to serve cold or to make Shepherd's Pie*.

BREAST OF LAMB: This extremely cheap cut of meat can provide a delicious main dish but frankly it can be most disappointing unless it is prepared with other ingredients which counteract the excessive fat content. A well-seasoned bread stuffing absorbs much of the extra fat and slow roasting of the stuffed and rolled breast draws out even more of the fat while keeping the joint juicy. To stew this cut successfully, some of the fat should be trimmed off, and the bones removed, before the meat is cut into smaller pieces. Certain other ingredients absorb and provide a contrast to the fat — root vegetables, sweetcorn kernels, any sort of soaked dried bean, or dried fruit. If the stew has a thick layer of fat on top when it is cooked, chill it, remove the solid fat and reheat the dish before serving.

LAMB AND MIXED VEGETABLE STEW

1 kg (2¼ lb) middle
  neck of lamb
25 g (1 oz) seasoned flour
2 tablespoons oil
450 ml (¾ pint) beef
  stock
4 sticks celery, chopped

2 large onions, chopped
2 medium carrots, sliced
½ teaspoon dried mixed
  herbs
225 g (8 oz) potato
  cubed

Coat the pieces of lamb in seasoned flour. Heat the oil in a pan and use to fry the lamb for 5 minutes, turning the pieces until sealed on all sides. Gradually mix in the stock and bring to the boil, stirring constantly. Add the celery, onion, carrot and herbs and cook gently for 1 hour, stirring occasionally. Add the potato, season with salt and pepper, cover and continue cooking for a further 45 minutes, or until the meat and vegetables are tender. Serves 4.

Variations:

Spiced Lamb Stew – Substitute 2 large sliced leeks, 1 small red pepper, deseeded and sliced, and 225 g (8 oz) diced swede for the celery, onion and carrot and use 1 teaspoon ground allspice instead of the herbs.

Fruited Lamb Stew – Substitute 8 small onions for the chopped onion, 225 g (8 oz) new potatoes for the cubed potato, and add 50 g (2 oz) dried apricots, soaked overnight then cut into strips. Omit the carrot and celery. Ten minutes before the stew is cooked, drain a 225 g (8 oz) can of butterbeans and add these to the mixture.

DEVILLED LAMB CHOPS WITH TOMATOES

4 *large loin or chump chops*	4 *tablespoons demerara sugar*
Salt and pepper	25 g (1 oz) *butter (or herbed butter*)*
4 *teaspoons French mustard*	4 *large tomatoes*

Season the chops with salt and pepper then take half the mustard and use to spread on one side of each chop. Sprinkle with half the sugar. Place the chops on a grid in the grill pan and cook under high heat for 10 minutes. Meanwhile, soften the butter, halve the tomatoes and cover the cut surfaces with butter. Turn the chops, spread with the remaining mustard and sprinkle with the rest of the sugar. Arrange the tomatoes on the rack with the chops and return to the grill for a further 10 minutes. Serve with creamed potatoes.
Serves 4.

SUPER SHEPHERD'S PIE

1 kg (2 lb) potatoes
150 ml ($\frac{1}{4}$ pint) thick
  well-seasoned gravy
450 g (1 lb) cooked
  lamb, minced

1 medium onion, minced
1 egg, beaten
Salt and pepper

Cook the potatoes in boiling salted water until tender. Meanwhile, place the gravy in a saucepan and mix in the meat and onion. Cook gently, stirring, for 3 minutes, then turn into an ovenproof pie dish. Drain the potatoes, mash until smooth then beat in almost all the egg and season well to taste with salt and pepper. Fork the potato over the meat mixture and brush the top with the remaining egg. Cook in a moderately hot oven (200°C, 400°F, Gas Mark 6) for 30 minutes, until well browned and crispy on top.
Serves 4.
Note: This is the best known, main dish using up left-over cooked meat and it can be made equally well with cooked beef or pork.

ROAST STUFFED PORK WITH APPLE SAUCE

1.5 kg (3 lb) boned hand
  of pork
1 packet sage and onion
  stuffing mix
1 egg, beaten
1 tablespoon oil

Salt and pepper
1 large cooking apple
2 tablespoons water
15 g ($\frac{1}{2}$ oz) butter
1 teaspoon sugar

Have the skin of the joint well scored. Make up the stuffing as instructed and stir in the egg. (If liked, add $\frac{1}{2}$ teaspoon dried mixed herbs.) Open up the pocket in the joint and fill with the stuffing mix. Tie the joint in a neat shape with string. Place in a roasting tin and rub the skin with oil and sprinkle with salt, then put into a cold oven to encourage the skin to form crackling. Set the oven temperature to moderately hot (190°C, 375°F, Gas

Mark 5) and calculate cooking time from the time the oven reaches the correct temperature, allowing 30 minutes per 450 g (1 lb) plus 30 minutes over. If any stuffing mixture is left over, form it into small balls with floured hands and place round the joint for the last 30 minutes of cooking time. To make the apple sauce, peel core and slice the apple. Place in a pan with the water and cook, covered, until the apple is pulpy. Beat in the butter and season with salt and pepper if liked (or add the sugar). Serve the joint sliced, with the stuffing and apple sauce.

Serves 4, with extra meat to serve cold.

SPARERIB CHOPS WITH HONEY GLAZE

*Finely grated rind and
juice of 1 orange*
*2 tablespoons clear
honey*
2 teaspoons soy sauce
*1 tablespoon tomato
purée*
1 chicken stock cube

*300 ml ($\frac{1}{2}$ pint) boiling
water*
1 tablespoon oil
*4 large pork sparerib
chops*
*2 tablespoons chopped
parsley*

Mix together the orange rind and juice, the honey, soy sauce, tomato purée, stock cube and water. Stir until well mixed. Heat the oil then use to fry the chops lightly on each side until golden. Pour in the sauce, bring to the boil, cover and simmer for 20 minutes. Arrange the chops and any sauce that remains on a warm serving dish and sprinkle with the parsley. Serve with freshly boiled ribbon noodles.

Serves 4.

SWEET AND SOUR PORK

*450 g (1 lb) boneless pork,
cubed*
Salt and pepper
2 tablespoons oil

1 teaspoon dry mustard
*600 ml (1 pint) chicken
stock*
2 tablespoons soft

SAUCE:
50 g (2 oz) butter
1 small onion, chopped
1 tablespoon flour

brown sugar
3 tablespoons vinegar
92 g (3¼ oz) can red
*   pimentoes*

Sprinkle the meat with salt and pepper. Heat the oil in a frying pan and use to fry the pork cubes gently for 10 minutes, stirring frequently, until cooked through and turning golden. Meanwhile, make the sauce. Melt the butter in a saucepan and use to fry the onion gently until soft. Stir in the flour and mustard and when well blended, gradually add the stock and bring to the boil, stirring constantly. Mix in the sugar, vinegar and liquid from the can of pimentoes then cut the pimentoes into strips and stir these in also. Boil gently for 5 minutes. Remove the pork cubes from the pan with a slotted draining spoon, add them to the sauce and simmer for a further 5 minutes. Serve with plenty of freshly cooked noodles.
Serves 4.

Variation:
Sweet and Sour Sausages – Substitute 450 g (1 lb) pork chipolata sausages for the pork cubes and fry these exactly the same way as above. Add to the sauce and simmer for only a further 3 minutes before serving.

GLAZED PORK AND MUSHROOM LOAF

350 g (12 oz) lean pork
100 g (4 oz) bacon,
*   derinded*
1 small onion, quartered
1 tablespoon chopped
*   parsley*
Salt and black pepper
2 eggs, beaten

175 g (6 oz) mushrooms
50 g (2 oz) Gouda cheese,
*   grated*
1 teaspoon oil
1 packet (300 ml (½ pint))
*   aspic jelly crystals*
300 ml (½ pint) boiling
*   water*

Mince together the pork, bacon and onion. Add the parsley and season with pepper and a little salt. Stir in the egg. Cut 5 neat slices of mushroom and reserve these for the garnish. Chop the remaining mushrooms. Place half the pork mixture in a greased

450 g (1 lb) loaf tin and cover with the mushrooms and cheese.
Press the rest of the pork mixture on top. Cover with foil and
cook in a moderate oven (180°C, 350°F, Gas Mark 4) for $1\frac{1}{2}$
hours. Leave to cool in the tin then turn out on a serving dish.
Sauté the reserved mushroom slices in the oil for 2 minutes.
Make up the aspic jelly crystals with the boiling water and allow
to cool until syrupy. Arrange the mushroom slices down the
centre of the loaf, then spoon over the aspic to glaze. Allow to set
before serving, cut into slices.
Serves 6.

LAMB'S LIVER HOT-POT

0.5 kg ($1\frac{1}{4}$ lb) potatoes
3 tablespoons oil
50 g (2 oz) butter
450 g (1 lb) lamb's liver,
  sliced
2 large carrots

1 medium onion, sliced
1 tablespoon flour
300 ml ($\frac{1}{2}$ pint) chicken
  stock
Salt and pepper
2 medium cooking
  apples

Thinly slice the potatoes and parboil in salted water to cover for
3 minutes. Meanwhile, heat 2 tablespoons of the oil and the
butter in a frying pan, add the liver slices and fry over high heat
for 1 minute on each side. Remove them from the pan. Thinly
slice the carrot and add to the juices remaining in the pan with
the onion. Fry gently until the onion just starts to soften. Stir in
the flour and when well blended, add the stock and bring to the
boil, stirring constantly. Season to taste with salt and pepper.
Peel, core and thinly slice the apples. Arrange the liver slices in
layers in an ovenproof dish with the onion mixture and apple.
Drain the potato slices and arrange, overlapping, on top of the
ingredients in the dish. Brush with the rest of the oil and bake in
a moderately hot oven (190°C, 375°F, Gas Mark 5) for 1 hour,
until the potato topping is golden brown and tender.
Serves 4–6.

SHERRIED KIDNEYS

0.5 kg (1¼ lb) ox kidney   2 tablespoons flour
25 g (1 oz) butter   450 ml (¾ pint) beef stock
2 tablespoons oil   3 tablespoons dry sherry
1 large onion, chopped   Salt and pepper

Remove skin and core from the kidney and cut into small pieces.
Heat the butter and oil in a saucepan and use to fry the onion
gently until beginning to soften. Add the kidney and fry, stirring, until it is sealed on all sides. Stir in the flour and when well
blended add the stock and sherry and bring to the boil, stirring
constantly. Season to taste, cover and simmer for 1 hour, or until
the kidney is tender. Check the seasoning and serve with
mashed potato.
Serves 4.

Variation:
Sherried Kidney in Rice Ring – Cook the kidney as above.
Meanwhile, cook 225 g (8 oz) long grain rice. Press the cooked
rice into a well-greased ring mould. Leave to stand for 1 minute
then turn out on a warm serving dish and turn the cooked
kidney into the centre.

PEANUT BUTTER CHICKEN

3 tablespoons oil   1 teaspoon salt
4 chicken portions   ½ teaspoon pepper
4 tablespoons tomato   4 tablespoons peanut
  purée   butter
300 ml (½ pint) water

Heat the oil in a large saucepan, put in the chicken portions and
fry until golden on both sides. Stir the tomato purée into the
water, pour over the chicken and sprinkle in the salt and pepper.
Bring to the boil, cover and simmer for 15 minutes. Blend the
peanut butter into the sauce in the pan, stir well, cover again and
cook for a further 20 minutes. Serve with fluffy boiled rice.
Serves 4.

CHICKEN PARCELS

2 rashers streaky bacon,
  derinded
1 small onion, chopped
50 g (2 oz) mushrooms,
  chopped

1 large tomato, chopped
Salt and pepper
2 chicken portions

Chop the bacon, mix with the onion, mushroom and tomato and season lightly with salt and pepper. Have ready 2 squares of foil, each large enough to enclose a chicken portion completely. Place a portion in the centre of each piece of foil, spoon over the bacon mixture and fold in the edges of the foil to make airtight parcels. Place the parcels on a baking sheet and cook in a moderately hot oven (190°C, 375°F, Gas Mark 5) for 50 minutes, opening the foil for the last 10 minutes of cooking time to allow the chicken to brown. Serve from the foil with small potatoes baked in the oven on the baking tray at the same time.
Serves 2.

SCOTCH FOWLIE

350 g (12 oz) leeks,
  trimmed
1 large onion, chopped
2 sticks celery, chopped
1.75 kg (4 lb) boiling
  fowl

50 g (2 oz) pearl barley
1 teaspoon finely grated
  lemon rind
2 chicken stock cubes
Salt and pepper

Cut the leeks into 2.5 cm (1 inch) lengths and wash well. Drain and place in a pan large enough to take the fowl and vegetables, with the onion, celery, the fowl and its giblets, the barley, lemon rind and sufficient water nearly to cover. Crumble in the stock cubes and bring to the boil. Season to taste with salt and pepper, cover and simmer for $2\frac{1}{2}$ –3 hours, or until the fowl is tender. Serve portions of the meat and pot vegetables with plenty of floury boiled potatoes.
Serves 6.
Note: This recipe produces sufficient well-flavoured stock to make soup as well for another day.

ALMOND CHICKEN OR TURKEY RECHAUFFÉ

225 g (8 oz) can water
  chestnuts, drained
1 medium onion, chopped
7.5 cm (3 inch) length
  cucumber, diced
100 g (4 oz) button
  mushrooms, halved

450 ml ($\frac{3}{4}$ pint) boiling
  chicken stock
3 tablespoons oil
450 g (1 lb) cooked chicken
  or turkey, cubed
1 tablespoon cornflour
Salt and pepper
50 g (2 oz) flaked almonds

Slice the water chestnuts and place in a pan with the onion,
cucumber and mushrooms. Pour over the hot stock and leave to
stand for 10 minutes. Meanwhile, heat 2 tablespoons of the oil
in a frying pan and use to stir-fry the cooked poultry for 2–3
minutes, until golden. Moisten the cornflour with 2 tablespoons
of the warm liquid from soaking the vegetables. Remove the
poultry pieces from the pan with a slotted draining spoon and
add to the vegetable mixture with the blended cornflour. Bring
to the boil, stirring constantly, until slightly thickened. Simmer
for 4 minutes and season to taste. Meanwhile, add the remaining oil to the frying pan and use to fry the almonds until just
golden. Turn the vegetable mixture into a serving dish and
sprinkle over the fried almonds.
Serves 4.

DUCK WITH OLIVES AND SHERRY

2.25 kg (5 lb) duck
300 ml ($\frac{1}{2}$ pint) water
Salt and pepper
3 tablespoons dry sherry

50 g (2 oz) drained stuffed
  green olives
1 tablespoon gravy
  powder

Roast the duck on a rack in a roasting tin in a moderately hot
oven (200°C, 400°F, Gas Mark 6) for 15 minutes per 450 g (1
lb) plus 15 minutes. Cook the giblets in the water with a little
seasoning for 20 minutes. Tip the duck so that the juices run out
of the carcase into the roasting tin then transfer the bird to a

warm serving dish, remove the rack from the roasting tin and spoon out excess fat (keep this for cooking as it is extremely well flavoured). Add the sherry to the juices left in the tin and stir over moderate heat for 1 minute. Add the olives and strain in the giblet stock. Moisten the gravy powder with 2 tablespoons cold water, add to the pan and cook over moderate heat, stirring constantly, until the sauce is smooth. Serve with the duck, boiled new potatoes and a green vegetable.
Serves 4.

ORANGE DUCK FOR TWO

1 orange
2 duck portions
Salt and pepper

1 tablespoon chunky
 orange marmalade
2 teaspoons cornflour

Finely grate the rind from the orange and squeeze the juice. Place the duck portions in a dish, pour over the orange juice and rind and sprinkle with salt and pepper. Allow to stand for at least 1 hour, turning the portions once during this time. Place the duck portions, skin side upwards, on a rack in a small roasting tin and pour over the marinade. Cook in a moderately hot oven (200°C, 400°F, Gas Mark 6) for 1 hour, basting halfway through cooking time with the juices in the tin. Remove the duck portions to a warm serving dish. Spoon out surplus fat and stir in the marmalade until melted. Moisten the cornflour with a little cold water, add to the pan and bring to the boil, stirring constantly. Simmer for 2–3 minutes and season to taste. Spoon over the duck portions and serve with boiled egg noodles.
Serves 2.

TURKEY LIVER AND BACON ROLLS

4 large turkey livers
8 rashers streaky bacon,
 derinded

1 tablespoon tomato
 ketchup
1 teaspoon oil
1 teaspoon soy sauce

77

Divide each turkey liver in half and use 1 rasher of bacon to wrap each piece of liver. Arrange the rolls on a greased baking sheet. (If they tend to unroll, secure each with a wooden cocktail stick for cooking then remove before serving.) Mix together the ketchup, oil and soy sauce and use to brush over the rolls. Cook in a moderately hot oven (200°C, 400°F, Gas Mark 6) for about 20 minutes, or until the bacon is crisp. The livers should be cooked but still just pink in the centres. Serve with fluffy boiled rice.

Serves 4.

Variation:

Chicken Liver Savoury – Use 8 chicken livers instead of the turkey livers and serve on hot buttered toast as a savoury course or snack.

ROAST TURKEY WITH RICE STUFFING

4.5 kg (10 lb) turkey	100 g (4 oz) long grain
450 g (1 lb) pork	rice
sausagemeat	300 ml ($\frac{1}{2}$ pint) water
Little oil	$\frac{1}{2}$ teaspoon salt
STUFFING:	$\frac{1}{4}$ teaspoon ground mace
25 g (1 oz) butter	$\frac{1}{2}$ teaspoon dried mixed
1 medium onion, chopped	herbs

First make the stuffing. Melt the butter in a pan and use to fry the onion gently until soft. Stir in the rice and fry for 1 minute. Add the water, salt, mace and herbs and bring to the boil. Stir once, cover and simmer for about 20 minutes, or until the rice is tender and has absorbed the liquid. Allow to cool. Remove the giblets from the turkey, stuff the neck end with the sausagemeat, shape neatly and smooth the flap of skin under the bird. Put the rice stuffing in the cavity and secure the opening with a small skewer. Put the bird into a roasting tin, brush with oil and cover with foil. Roast in a moderate oven (160°C, 325°F, Gas Mark 3) for $3\frac{1}{2}$ hours. Remove the foil, baste the bird with the juices in the tin and cook, uncovered, for a further 30 minutes, to brown the skin. Serve with roast potatoes, Brussels sprouts and cranberry sauce.

Serves 8, with extra meat to serve cold.

BACON SLIPPER STEW

0.75 kg (1½ lb) boneless
  slipper of bacon
50 g (2 oz) dried apricots
2 tablespoons oil
1 large onion, chopped
225 g (8 oz) parsnip,
  diced
2 large carrots, sliced

1 teaspoon French
  mustard
600 ml (1 pint) chicken
  stock
450 g (1 lb) potatoes,
  cubed
1 tablespoon cornflour
Salt and pepper

Soak the piece of bacon and the apricots separately in cold water to cover overnight. Drain the bacon and cut the meat into cubes. Drain and snip the apricots into strips. Heat the oil in a large pan and use to fry the onion, parsnip and carrot gently until the onion starts to soften. Add the pieces of bacon and fry, stirring, until they are sealed on all sides. Add the apricots, mustard and chicken stock and bring to the boil. Stir well, cover and simmer for 30 minutes. Add the potato, bring back to simmering point, cover again and cook on for a further 30 minutes, or until the potato is tender. Moisten the cornflour with a little cold water, add to the stew and bring back to the boil, stirring constantly. Simmer for 2 minutes and season to taste with salt and pepper. Serves 4.

Variation:

Bacon Slipper Stew with Beans – Omit the potato and allow the stew to cook for 1 hour. Drain 425 g (15 oz) can of cannellini beans and add to the stew before thickening.

BOILED BACON WITH RAISIN SAUCE

1–1.5 kg (2–3 lb) joint
  collar or forehock of

¾ teaspoon dry mustard
1½ teaspoons cornflour

bacon
SAUCE:
200 ml (6 fl oz) water
25 g (1 oz) soft brown
sugar

4 teaspoons vinegar
40 g (1½ oz) seedless
raisins
15 g (½ oz) butter

Soak the joint in cold water to cover for 2 hours. Drain and place in a saucepan with fresh water to cover, bring to the boil, cover the pan and simmer for 20 minutes per 450 g (1 lb) plus 20 minutes over. Meanwhile, make the sauce. Place the water, sugar and mustard in a small pan and stir well. Mix together the cornflour and vinegar, add to the pan with the raisins and butter and bring to the boil, stirring all the time. Simmer for 10 minutes. Lift out the joint and place on a serving dish. Strip off the rind and serve the meat sliced with boiled potatoes and green peas and hand the sauce separately.

Serves 4, with extra meat to serve cold.

Note: The stock from cooking the bacon is very tasty and is ideal to use as part of the liquid required for making soup. Check the saltiness and make up the total quantity required with water.

Variations:

Cold Boiled Bacon – When the joint is cooked, remove from the pan and strip off the rind. Press 50 g (2 oz) toasted breadcrumbs carefully into the fat on the joint and allow to cool.

Mustard Glazed Bacon – When the rind has been removed, score the fat into diamonds. Spread 1 teaspoon French mustard over the top and sprinkle with 1 tablespoon demerara sugar. Place in a roasting tin and bake in a moderately hot oven (190°C, 375°F, Gas Mark 5) for about 10 minutes, until the surface is golden and bubbling. Serve hot or cold.

GRILLED GAMMON WITH APRICOTS

4 gammon steaks
225 g (8 oz) can apricot
halves

1 tablespoon oil

Snip the fat on the gammon steaks if necessary, to prevent them curling up. Place on a grid in the grill pan. Take 2 tablespoons of the syrup from the can of apricots and mix with the oil. Use a little of this mixture to brush the steaks and grill them under high heat for 4 minutes. Turn the steaks, brush again with the syrup mixture and grill for 3 minutes. (Drain the remaining syrup from the apricots and reserve to use later, possibly in a fruit salad.) Arrange the apricots on the gammon steaks, brush them with the syrup mixture and return the pan to the grill for a further 1−2 minutes, until the fruit is hot and turning golden. Serve with freshly boiled pasta shells and a green salad.

Serves 4.

Note: Canned peach slices or pineapple rings can be used instead of the apricots.

Vegetable Cookery

MUNG BEAN SPROUTS WITH CARROTS

These sprouting beans are rich in Vitamin C, and can be grown in a little water at any time of the year. Soak 1 cup dried mung beans in water for 2–3 days. Once the sprouts appear, spread the beans evenly between 2 layers of blotting paper and place in a large rectangular dish. Moisten the blotting paper with water each day (it should always be damp), and keep in a dark warm place. Once the sprouts are 2.5 cm (1 inch) long and plump they are ready to use.

225 g (8 oz) bean sprouts
  (grown as above)
1 small onion, chopped
50 g (2 oz) butter
225 g (8 oz) carrots,
  grated

grated rind and juice of
  $\frac{1}{2}$ orange
Pinch of ground ginger
Salt and pepper

Put the bean sprouts into a bowl of cold water and wait for the shells or 'hoods' to float to the surface. Remove these and cut off the roots from each sprout. Fry the onion gently in the butter until soft. Add the remaining ingredients, including the prepared sprouts and a little seasoning. Cover and cook for 2 minutes. Serve immediately. This vegetable mixture makes a tasty accompaniment to chicken and pork dishes.
Serves 4.

CHINESE LEAVES WITH CRAB MEAT SAUCE

450 g (1 lb) Chinese
  leaves
4 tablespoons oil
1 clove garlic, crushed

2 tablespoons dry sherry
1 tablespoon cornflour
300 ml ($\frac{1}{2}$ pint) chicken
  stock

225 g (8 oz) fresh or   Salt and pepper
  canned crab meat

Finely shred the Chinese leaves. Heat the oil in a large shallow
pan. Add the Chinese leaves and the garlic and stir over brisk
heat for 3 minutes. Remove the Chinese leaves to a plate and
keep warm. Add the crab meat and sherry to the fat remaining in
the pan and cook for 1 minute. Blend the cornflour with the
chicken stock and stir into the pan. Cook for 1 minute until the
crab sauce thickens and clears, stirring gently. Fold the Chinese
leaves into the sauce and heat through for 1 minute. Season to
taste with salt and pepper and serve immediately.
Serves 4.
Variation:
Chinese Leaves with Tuna Sauce – Drain and flake a 200 g (7 oz)
can of tuna and use in place of the crab meat.

FRENCH-STYLE PEAS

50 g (2 oz) butter   1 lettuce heart, shredded
1 tablespoon oil   4 tablespoons double
1 large onion, chopped   cream
1 clove garlic, crushed   Salt and pepper
4 rashers bacon, chopped
225 g (8 oz) frozen peas,
  thawed

Heat the butter and the oil in a large shallow pan and use to fry
the onion gently for 3 minutes. Add the garlic and bacon and
cook for a further 2 minutes. Put in the peas, cover the pan and
cook for 3 minutes. Stir in the lettuce, cream and salt and pepper
to taste. Heat through until piping hot.
Serves 4.
Variation:
Creamed Sweetcorn and Peas – Omit the cream and stir the contents of a 298 g (10 $\frac{1}{2}$ oz) can of creamed sweetcorn into the bacon
mixture as above.

RATATOUILLE

1 large aubergine,
  (about 225 g (8 oz))
225 g (8 oz) courgettes
Salt and pepper
225 g (8 oz) tomatoes,
  peeled
1 small sweet red
  pepper, deseeded

1 small sweet green
  pepper, deseeded
3 tablespoons olive oil
2 medium onions, sliced
2 cloves garlic, crushed
1 teaspoon dried basil
1 tablespoon lemon
  juice

Cut the aubergine and courgettes into thin slices and arrange in a colander, sprinkling them lightly with salt. Leave to drain for 30 minutes, then dry the vegetable slices on absorbent kitchen paper. Chop the tomatoes and cut the peppers into strips. Heat the oil in a large pan and use to fry the onion and garlic gently until soft. Add the aubergine and courgette slices and the pepper strips and stir well. Cover and cook gently for 20 minutes. Add the tomato, basil and lemon juice, season well and bring to the boil, stirring. Cover and simmer for a further 30 minutes, or until the vegetables are soft but not reduced to a purée. Adjust the seasoning and serve hot or cold as a starter. Serves 4.
Note: For parties add a few black olives just before the end of cooking time.

STEAMED LEEKS AND COURGETTES

2 large leeks
6 medium courgettes
Salt and pepper
75 g (3 oz) butter
Good pinch of ground
  nutmeg

1 teaspoon dried mixed
  herbs
1 tablespoon chopped
  parsley

Trim the leeks and courgettes. Wash thoroughly and drain. Cut into 0.5 cm ($\frac{1}{4}$ inch) slices. Place the vegetables in a metal colander and season to taste. Cover with a plate or lid and steam over simmering water for about 20 minutes, or until just tender. Meanwhile, heat the butter with the nutmeg, mixed herbs, parsley and salt and pepper to taste. Put the steamed vegetables into a warm serving dish and spoon over the hot flavoured butter.

Serves 4.

Variation:

Leeks and Courgettes au Gratin — Put the steamed vegetables into a greased ovenproof dish and top with 2 tablespoons dried breadcrumbs and 75 g (3 oz) grated cheese. Brown under a hot grill before serving.

FENNEL IN CREAM SAUCE

4 *small heads of fennel*	150 *ml* ($\frac{1}{4}$ *pint*) *chicken stock*
25 *g* (1 *oz*) *butter*	*Salt and pepper*
2 *tablespoons oil*	150 *ml* ($\frac{1}{4}$ *pint*) *double*
1 *small onion, finely*	*cream*
chopped	2 *tablespoons chopped*
1 *tablespoon lemon juice*	*parsley*

Trim the heads of fennel and cut each one in half lengthways. Heat the butter and oil in a large shallow pan and use to fry the onion gently until soft. Arrange the pieces of fennel in a single layer in the pan and pour over the lemon juice and stock and season to taste. Cover and cook gently for 20–25 minutes, or until the fennel is just tender. Remove the fennel to a serving dish and keep warm. Boil the juices remaining in the pan until reduced by half. Stir in the cream and parsley and heat through gently. Pour the hot creamy sauce over the fennel and serve immediately.

Serves 4.

Variation:

Celery in Creamy Sauce — Trim 1 head of celery and cut the sticks into even-sized lengths. Wash, drain and cook as above.

BAKED CHEESY AUBERGINES

2 large aubergines
  (total about 450 g
  (1 lb))
Salt and pepper
2 eggs, beaten
75 g (3 oz) dried
  breadcrumbs

150 ml ($\frac{1}{4}$ pint) olive oil
100 g (4 oz) Gruyère
  cheese, sliced
4 tablespoons tomato
  purée
50 g (2 oz) grated
  Parmesan cheese

Slice the aubergines quite thinly. Put the slices in a colander, sprinkle generously with salt and leave to stand and drain for 30 minutes. Pat the slices dry, then dip them into beaten egg and cover all over in breadcrumbs, to give a thin even coating. Heat the olive oil in a large shallow pan and fry the aubergine slices on both sides until pale golden. Drain on absorbent paper. Arrange alternate layers of aubergine, Gruyère cheese, tomato purée and Parmesan in a greased ovenproof dish, finishing with a layer of cheese. Bake in a moderately hot oven (190°C, 375°F, Gas Mark 5) for 25–30 minutes, until golden brown on top. Serve hot with a salad.
Serves 4–6.

FRIED LENTIL CAKES

225 g (8 oz) lentils
1 clove garlic, crushed
1 tablespoon chopped
  fresh mint

Salt and pepper
Oil for deep frying

Soak the lentils in cold water overnight – make sure that there is plenty of water to cover the lentils as they swell considerably. Drain well and liquidise with the garlic, mint and seasoning to taste until smooth. Squeeze the purée in a piece of muslin to remove excess moisture. On a well-floured surface, shape into round flat cakes about 7.5 cm (3 inches) in diameter and 2.5 cm (1 inch) thick. Using a small biscuit cutter, cut a hole in the centre of each cake. (They will look like American doughnuts.)

Gather these cut-outs together and shape them also. Deep fry the lentil cakes in hot oil for 5–6 minutes, or until crisp, golden brown and cooked through. Drain on absorbent paper and serve hot with fruit chutney.

Serves 4.

Variation:

Lentil Cakes with Meat – Add 100 g (4 oz) finely chopped chicken or ham to the lentil purée, before moulding it into cakes.

SPICED CAULIFLOWER PURÉE

1 large cauliflower	$\frac{1}{2}$ teaspoon ground ginger
2 large onions, chopped	2 teaspoons dry mustard
3 cloves garlic, crushed	$\frac{1}{2}$ teaspoon salt
75 g (3 oz) butter	$\frac{1}{2}$ teaspoon ground black
1 teaspoon ground turmeric	pepper
1 tablespoon ground coriander	4 tablespoons natural yogurt
2 teaspoons ground cumin	150 ml ($\frac{1}{4}$ pint) chicken stock

Trim off the leaves and excess stalk from the cauliflower and chop the florets finely. Fry the onion and garlic in the butter until soft. Add the spices and seasonings and cook for 1 further minute. Put in the cauliflower and cook until it is pale golden. Stir in the yogurt and stock and cook gently until the cauliflower is tender and has formed a velvety purée. This purée is equally good served hot or chilled.

Serves 4.

EASY HOME-MADE SAUERKRAUT

1 kg ($2\frac{1}{4}$ lb) white cabbage	1 bay leaf
75 g (3 oz) sea salt	2 teaspoons caraway seeds
1 tablespoon lemon juice	
1 large onion, chopped	3 tablespoons wine vinegar
3 tablespoons oil	

1 clove garlic, crushed
6 juniper berries, crushed
½ teaspoon ground black
   pepper

200 ml (7 fl oz) chicken
   stock

Finely shred, wash and drain the cabbage. Place in a large bowl
and mix in the salt and lemon juice. Cover with a weighted plate
and leave to stand for 2 hours. Rinse the cabbage in cold water
and squeeze out as much moisture as possible with your hands.
Fry the onion in the oil until soft. Add the garlic and cabbage
and fry gently for 10 minutes, turning frequently. Add the
remaining ingredients, stir well and cook gently until the sauer-
kraut is tender and has turned pinkish-brown.
Serves 6.
Note: Serve with frankfurters, boiling ring sausage, or bacon
joints.

SPINACH AND MUSHROOM TOASTS

0.75 g (1½ lb) fresh
   spinach
50 g (2 oz) butter
Salt and pepper
Pinch of ground nutmeg
175 g (6 oz) button
   mushrooms

2 tablespoons lemon
   juice
4 slices freshly-made
   toast
75 g (3 oz) cream cheese
3 tablespoons grated
   Parmesan cheese

Wash the spinach thoroughly, trimming off any tough stalks.
Shake dry and place in a pan with half the butter, salt and
pepper to taste, and the nutmeg. Cover the pan and cook gently
for about 10 minutes, until the spinach is just tender. Drain the
spinach, chop roughly and keep warm. Meanwhile, cook the
mushrooms in the remaining butter and the lemon juice. Spread
each slice of toast with cream cheese, top with spinach, then
mushrooms, and a generous sprinkling of Parmesan. Pop under
a hot grill for about 2 minutes and serve immediately.
Serves 4.
Variation:
Beetroot Tops and Mushroom Toasts – Substitute young leaves
from beetroot for the spinach.

Rice and Pasta

RICE

There are now various kinds of long grain rice available, including pre-cooked rice, so it is important to note the directions given on the pack for the length of time it takes to cook. Brown rice is the whole unpolished grain, with only the outer hull and some bran removed, so it retains more of the natural food values, but it takes about 40 minutes cooking in plenty of boiling salted water to become tender.

HOW TO COOK RICE

Here are some general instructions for cooking long grain white American and Patna rice by the double-up method, which produces a good result without the necessity of using a large saucepan. Put 225 g (8 oz) long grain rice and 1 teaspoon salt into the pan. Add 600 ml (1 pint) water. (For smaller quantities fill a small cup with rice and allow 2 cups of water, with less salt.) Bring to the boil and stir once. Cover the pan and simmer for 15 minutes, or until the rice is tender and has absorbed all the water. For the 'easy cook' type of rice, allow 175 g (6 oz) only of rice to 600 ml (1 pint) water to end up with the same cooked quantity. This produces 0.75 kg (1½ lb) cooked rice and is ample to serve 4. Basmati rice has a very small grain and remains firm in texture even when fully cooked. Round-grain pudding rice has a floury texture and is more suited to long cooking in milk for sweet dishes.

HOW TO STORE COOKED RICE

Sometimes there is some loose rice flour with the grains, and it is worth turning the cooked rice into a sieve and pouring fresh hot water through it to clear this. Drain well, cool and place the rice in a strong polythene bag or container without compressing it too much. Seal and store in the refrigerator for up to 3 days. To reheat, return to a saucepan, add 1 tablespoon water and place over a moderate heat, shaking rather than stirring which breaks up the grains, until piping hot. To freeze cooked rice, store in the container for up to 3 months. To reheat frozen rice, allow to defrost, spread in an ovenproof dish, dot with butter, cover with foil and place in a moderate oven (180°C, 350°F, Gas Mark 4) for 15 minutes.

PRESENTATION OF RICE

It is very easy to serve rice in spectacular ways. Saffron is expensive, but golden rice need not necessarily be cooked in water coloured with it. Use ground turmeric or yellow food colouring instead. To add colour to a dish of snowy cooked rice, speckle the surface with finely-chopped parsley or sweet paprika pepper. Cooked rice is very easy to mould. Pack it into coffee cups, tea cups or a ring mould, oiled or rinsed out with hot water. Press down lightly, allow to stand for 1 minute, then turn out. Diced canned pimento or green peas can be added to make the rice moulds more colourful.

FRIED RICE

2 tablespoons oil
2 eggs, beaten
0.75 kg (1½ lb) cold
  cooked rice
50 g (2 oz) button
  mushrooms, sliced

4 spring onions, chopped
100 g (4 oz) ham, diced
1 tablespoon soy sauce

Heat the oil in a large heavy pan and pour in the egg. Cook, stirring with a fork, until it just begins to set. Put in the rice and keep stirring over gentle heat, gradually adding the mushrooms, onion and ham, until the mixture is piping hot. Fork through the soy sauce and serve hot.
Serves 4.

Note: This recipe can be elaborated by adding other ingredients such as cooked green peas, sweetcorn kernels and chopped prawns.

RISOTTO

25 g (1 oz) butter
1 tablespoon oil
1 small onion, chopped
225 g (8 oz) long grain
   rice

600 ml (1 pint) chicken
   stock
Salt and black pepper
50–100 g (2–4 oz) grated
   Parmesan cheese

Heat the butter and oil in a saucepan and use to fry the onion gently until soft. Stir in the rice and fry for 2 minutes. Add the stock and bring to the boil. Stir once, cover the pan and simmer for 15–20 minutes without stirring. The rice should be tender and the liquid absorbed. If necessary, cook on for a further few minutes then fluff up with a fork, season with salt and black pepper and serve with the cheese. The amount of cheese to be added is decided by whether you intend to serve the dish as a main meal or as a snack.

Serves 4.

Note: If using Italian instead of long grain rice, more liquid will be required – up to another 300 ml ($\frac{1}{2}$ pint) – before the rice is tender.

Variation:

Chicken Liver Risotto – Cut 225 g (8 oz) chicken livers in half and add to the fat with the rice. Fry, stirring, until firm then add 2 tablespoons dry sherry with the stock and continue cooking as above. Serve with just a sprinkling of cheese.

PILAFF

1 medium onion
2 tablespoons oil
225 g (8 oz) long grain
   rice

600 ml (1 pint) strong
   chicken stock
Salt and pepper
1 tablespoon chopped
   parsley

Finely chop the onion. Heat the oil in a medium saucepan and use to cook the onion gently until soft. Stir in the rice and fry for 2 minutes. Season the stock with salt and pepper to taste, add to the saucepan and bring to the boil. Stir well and transfer to an ovenproof dish. Cover and cook in a moderately hot oven (190°C, 375°F, Gas Mark 5) for 45 minutes. Fluff up the rice and sprinkle with the parsley before serving.

Serves 4.

Note: The flavour of the pilaff can be altered by adding a little ground spice to the cooking liquid. Try 1 teaspoon ground ginger, $\frac{1}{2}$ teaspoon ground allspice or 1 teaspoon ground coriander.

Variation:

Persian Pilaff – To turn the above into a complete meal, add 175 g (6 oz) shredded cooked chicken, 50 g (2 oz) seedless raisins and 1 tablespoon flaked almonds when you put the rice into the dish. Lay 2 bay leaves and 1 cinnamon stick lightly on the surface before cooking. The pilaff gives off a delightful oriental aroma when you remove the lid from the dish at serving time.

PASTA

Good quality pasta is made with semolina milled from hard durum wheat. You can choose ordinary pasta which itself has a significant protein value and is highly nutritious; or enriched pasta which has had egg added to give an attractive golden colour and a slightly more delicate flavour. Wholewheat pasta, with its richer colour and nutty flavour, is the obvious choice for people who are conscious of the advantages of a high fibre diet. Green pasta is coloured by the addition of spinach, and is paler when cooked than when seen raw in the packet. Not all the many shapes available are to be had in enriched or green pasta or even in wholewheat pasta, but cooking instructions are indicated on the pack, and usually the length of cooking time varies according to the size and density of the shape.

HOW TO COOK PASTA

A fairly large pan is always needed because pasta trebles both in weight and volume by the time it is cooked. For example, allow 2.25 litres (4 pints) lightly salted boiling water to cook each 225 g (8 oz) pasta. A teaspoon or two of oil added to the cooking water prevents the pieces from sticking together. Turn in 'shapes' all at once or coil in lengths of spaghetti as the ends soften. Whatever the instructions, stir once or twice to keep the pieces separate and taste for yourself to make sure the pasta is cooked as you like it. Drain in a colander. A few drops of oil sprinkled over the pasta in the colander gives it a gloss for serving.

225 g (8 oz) raw pasta produces sufficient for 4 portions.

HOW TO STORE COOKED PASTA

Run cold water through it in the colander, drain well and place in a strong polythene bag or container. As with rice, do not compress it. Seal and store in the refrigerator for up to 4 days, or in the freezer for up to 3 months. To reheat, turn the pasta into a pan of boiling water and as soon as the water comes to the boil again, drain and serve. Use the same method for reheating pasta straight from the freezer. Gently stir to separate as the pasta reheats, otherwise the outer pieces will become overcooked before the water returns to the boil.

PRESENTATION OF PASTA

The classic Italian way to eat pasta is to serve it freshly cooked on individual plates piled up and topped with a rich sauce. The sauce must be concentrated and flavourful as it has to complement the bland taste of the pasta itself. However, perfectly cooked pasta makes a good meal lightly tossed with a little olive oil and sprinkled generously with freshly ground black pepper and grated Parmesan cheese or finely chopped parsley. Extra cheese is handed separately. For modern tastes, the added excitement of grated lemon rind, finely chopped black olives or strips of red and green sweet pepper might be preferred.

Leftover cooked pasta takes on a second lease of life when it is deep fried. It makes an attractive garnish for cream soups or any dish where you might otherwise use croûtons. Heat a minimum of 5 cm (2 inches) of oil to moderately hot. Test by putting in one piece of pasta which should sizzle at once and become golden brown within 30 seconds. Make sure the pasta is really dry, if necessary patting it between two layers of absorbent kitchen paper. Fry small quantities at a time, using a wire frying basket or removing the pasta from the pan with a slotted draining spoon when brown. Drain well before serving.

CHICKEN STUFFED CANNELLONI

225 g (8 oz) cannelloni	Good pinch dried mixed
1 medium onion, chopped	herbs
50 g (2 oz) mushrooms,	175 g (6 oz) cooked
chopped	chicken, diced
3 tablespoons oil	6 tablespoons milk
½ chicken stock cube	283 g (10 oz) can
4 tablespoons hot water	condensed celery soup
1 egg, beaten	
2 tablespoons fresh	
breadcrumbs	

Cook the cannelloni and drain well. Meanwhile, fry the onion and mushrooms in the oil until the onion is soft. Make up the stock cube with the hot water and whisk in the egg. Stir the breadcrumbs, herbs and chicken into the onion mixture, then the egg stock. Slit each cannelloni down one side, open out and fill with some of the chicken mixture. Roll up and arrange close together in a greased ovenproof dish. Beat the milk into the soup, pour over the cannelloni and cook in a moderate oven (180°C, 350°F, Gas Mark 4) for 30 minutes.

Serves 4.

Variation:
Tuna Stuffed Cannelloni – Substitute a 198 g (7 oz) can of tuna, including the liquid in the can, for the chicken and add 25 g (1 oz) chopped stuffed green olives. Omit the mushrooms and stock.

LASAGNE VERDI

175 g (6 oz) lasagne
  verdi
225 g (8 oz) can tomatoes
1 quantity All Purpose
  Bolognese Sauce*

300 ml ($\frac{1}{2}$ pint) hot
  cheese sauce*
25 g (1 oz) Cheddar
  cheese, grated

Arrange half the dry lasagne, in a single layer, in a greased shallow ovenproof dish. Chop the tomatoes and stir into the mince with the liquid from the can. Spoon half the mixture over the lasagne. Spoon half the sauce over the mince. Repeat the layers once more. Sprinkle with the cheese and bake in a moderate oven (180°C, 350°F, Gas Mark 4) for 45 minutes. Serves 4.
Variation:
Baked Bean Lasagne – Chop 1 large onion and fry in 2 table-spoons oil until soft. Stir in a 425 g (15 oz) can baked beans and use instead of the savoury mince.

RICH RICE OR PASTA PUDDING

75 g (3 oz) pudding rice
  or small pasta shapes
600 ml (1 pint) milk
Pinch of salt
2 egg yolks

50 g (2 oz) castor sugar
15 g ($\frac{1}{2}$ oz) butter
Little ground nutmeg or
  cinnamon

Simmer the rice or pasta in the milk with the salt for about 20 minutes, until soft. Beat the egg yolks with the sugar and stir into the hot mixture. Turn into a buttered pie dish, dot with the butter and sprinkle with spice. Bake in a moderate oven (180°C,

350°F, Gas Mark 4) for 25 minutes, or until golden brown on top.

Serves 4.

Variations:

Sunday Best Milk Pudding — Substitute 1 small can evaporated milk for an equal quantity of the fresh milk and stir 50 g (2 oz) sultanas and 1 teaspoon grated lemon rind into the hot mixture before baking.

Meringue Milk Pudding — Bake the pudding as given in the main recipe for 20 minutes only. Spread 3 tablespoons warm jam over the surface. Whisk 2 egg whites until stiff and gradually whisk in 3 tablespoons castor sugar until the meringue is glossy and thick. Spoon or pipe over the jam and return to the oven for a further 10–15 minutes until the meringue is golden brown.

Pastry

BASIC FORK-MIX SHORTCRUST PASTRY

*150 g (5 oz) soft
  margarine*

*4 tablespoons water
275 g (10 oz) plain flour*

Put the margarine, water and 4 tablespoons of the flour in a
bowl and mix with a fork until blended. Gradually add the
remaining flour and continue to mix with the fork until a dough
forms. Turn out on a floured surface and knead lightly until
smooth. Best chilled for 30 minutes before use.
Yield: about 450 g (1 lb) pastry.
(Suitable alternatives to using all soft margarine are half soft
margarine, and half soft lard or whipped vegetable fat.)
Variations:
Wholewheat Pastry – Substitute wholewheat flour for half the
plain flour and add an extra 2 teaspoons of water.

SAUSAGE AND APPLE PLATE PIE

*350 g (12 oz) basic
  shortcrust pastry*
1 small onion, grated
$\frac{1}{2}$ teaspoon dried sage
Salt and pepper*

*350 g (12 oz) pork
  sausagemeat
1 medium cooking apple
Beaten egg to glaze*

Roll out half the pastry and line a 20 cm (8 inch) pie plate. Work
the onion, sage and a little seasoning into the sausagemeat and
then divide into two equal quantities. Shape each portion into a
thin round and place one in the pastry case. Peel, core and slice
the apple and arrange the slices evenly on the sausagemeat.
Cover with the remaining round of sausagemeat. Brush the
exposed pastry edges with beaten egg. Roll out the rest of the
pastry to make a lid, lift over the filling, seal the edges well

together and flute them. Cut a steam vent in the pastry top, brush the pie with beaten egg and cut decorations such as leaves from the pastry trimmings. Brush these also with egg. Bake in a moderately hot oven (200°C, 400°F, Gas Mark 6) for 30 minutes, then reduce the heat to moderate (160°C, 325°F, Gas Mark 3) and continue cooking for a further 30 minutes.
Serves 4–6.

CORNISH PASTIES

350 g (12 oz) basic
  shortcrust pastry*
225 g (8 oz) potato
1 medium onion
175 g (6 oz) beef skirt

$\frac{1}{2}$ beef stock cube
4 tablespoons boiling
  water
Pinch of black pepper
Beaten egg to glaze

Roll out the pastry and cut into four rounds using a small plate as a guide. Coarsely grate the potato and onion and finely chop the meat. Make up the stock cube with the boiling water and combine with the meat, potato, onion and pepper. Divide between the pastry rounds. Bring up the sides of each pastry round to meet over the filling, brush with beaten egg, seal the edges well together and flute them. Place on a greased baking sheet and bake in a hot oven (220°C, 425°F, Gas Mark 7) for 10 minutes then reduce heat to moderate (180°C, 350°F, Gas Mark 4) and continue cooking for a further 30 minutes.
Makes 4.

BAKEWELL TART

225 g (8 oz) basic
  shortcrust pastry*
2 tablespoons raspberry
  jam
25 g (1 oz) ground
  almonds

1 tablespoon milk
Few drops almond essence
1 egg quantity All-in-
  One Victoria sandwich
  mix*
Icing sugar to sprinkle

Roll out the pastry and use to line a 17.5 cm (7 inch) sandwich tin. Spread the jam in the bottom. Stir the almonds, milk and almond essence into the cake mixture until well blended then spread evenly over the jam. Bake in a moderately hot oven (190°C, 375°F, Gas Mark 5) for about 40 minutes, or until golden brown. Allow to cool and sprinkle with icing sugar before serving.

Serves 4-6.

Variation:

Syrup Tart - Line sandwich tin with pastry as above. Warm 225 g (8 oz) golden syrup with 25 g (1 oz) margarine until fat melts. Stir in 50 g (2 oz) fresh breadcrumbs and 2 tablespoons lemon juice. Spread in pastry case and bake in a moderately hot oven (200°C, 400°F, Gas Mark 6) for 30 minutes.

HAM AND CHEESE QUICHE

350 g (12 oz) basic shortcrust pastry*	100 g (4 oz) Cheddar cheese, grated
1 small onion, chopped	2 eggs
15 g ($\frac{1}{2}$ oz) butter	300 ml ($\frac{1}{2}$ pint) milk
100 g (4 oz) lean ham, chopped	Salt and black pepper

Roll out the pastry and use to line a 27.5 cm (9 inch) flan tin. Fry the onion gently in the butter until soft. Spoon evenly into the pastry case, scatter over the pieces of ham and the cheese. Beat the eggs with the milk and season well. Pour carefully over the filling ingredients and bake in a moderately hot oven (200°C, 400°F, Gas Mark 6) for 35 minutes, or until the filling is set and the top golden brown.

Serves 4-6.

Variation:

Seafood Quiche - Line flan tin with pastry as above. Drain and flake a 99 g ($3\frac{1}{2}$ oz) can tuna, reserving the oil, and arrange in pastry case with 50 g (2 oz) shelled prawns. Beat 2 eggs with the tuna oil, 300 ml ($\frac{1}{2}$ pint) milk, pinch of ground nutmeg, salt and pepper. Pour into quiche and bake as above.

Economy tip: Substitute a 43 g ($1\frac{1}{2}$ oz) can of dressed crab for the prawns.

FRENCH APPLE FLAN

350 g (12 oz) basic
   shortcrust pastry*
450 ml ($\frac{3}{4}$ pint) thick
   apple purée
Castor sugar to taste
3 dessert apples, cored

4 tablespoons lemon
   juice
2 tablespoons apricot
   jam
2 tablespoons water

Roll out the pastry and use to line a 27.5 cm (9 inch) flan tin.
Line with greaseproof paper, fill with baking beans and bake
'blind' in a moderately hot oven (190°C, 375°F, Gas Mark 5)
for 10 minutes. Sweeten the apple purée to taste and spread in
the pastry case. Peel the apples and cut into neat slices. Toss
them lightly with half the lemon juice until coated then arrange
in concentric circles, overlapping, on top of the apple purée.
Bake in the oven for 25 minutes, or until apples are tender and
just turning golden brown. Cool. Mash the jam with the
remaining lemon juice and the water and heat, stirring, until
well blended. Press through a sieve and while it is still warm,
brush over the apple topping to glaze.
Serves 6.

PUFF PASTRY

As the method for making this type of pastry is extremely
complicated it is advisable to use bought frozen puff pastry.

STEAK AND KIDNEY PIE

275 g (10 oz) frozen
   puff pastry, defrosted

0.75 kg (1$\frac{1}{2}$ lb) cooked steak
   and kidney in gravy, cold
Beaten egg to glaze

Roll out the pastry to the shape of a 1 litre (1$\frac{3}{4}$ pint) pie dish and
about 2.5 cm (1 inch) larger all round. Cut off a strip of pastry
wide enough to cover the rim of the dish, dampen it and press it
on. Put a pie funnel in the centre of the dish. Pour in the meat

mixture and brush the pastry rim with water. Lift over the pastry lid, press to seal and raise the edge by cutting horizontally with the sharp blade of a knife. Leave in a cool place for 30 minutes then brush with beaten egg and bake in a hot oven (220°C, 425°F, Gas Mark 7) for 35–40 minutes, or until well browned.
Serves 4–6.

PORK FILLET EN CROÛTE

75 g (3 oz) packet parsley and thyme stuffing mix	1 tablespoon oil 450 g (1 lb) frozen puff pastry, defrosted
Boiling water 2 small pork fillets	Beaten egg to glaze

Make up the stuffing mix with the boiling water as directed. Spread half the stuffing on the larger pork fillet, top with the smaller fillet and tie them together firmly to enclose the stuffing. Place on a baking sheet, brush with oil and cook in a moderately hot oven (200°C, 400°F, Gas Mark 6) for 30 minutes. Cool and remove the string. Roll out the pastry to a rectangle large enough to completely enclose the fillets, lift them into the centre of it and press the remaining stuffing around them. Bring up the pastry to make a neat parcel of the fillets, brush all edges with beaten egg and press well to seal. Place on a damped baking sheet with the seal downwards. Cut decorations from the pastry trimmings, brush with beaten egg and stick on the top of the roll. Chill for 30 minutes. Brush all over with beaten egg and bake in a hot oven (230°C, 450°F, Gas Mark 8) for 15 minutes, until the pastry is just golden then reduce the heat to moderately hot (190°C, 375°F, Gas Mark 5) and cook for a further 15–20 minutes, until rich golden brown.
Serves 4.

Beef Wellington is a luxury version of this recipe using a fillet of beef enclosed in a cooked mushroom mixture or liver pâté before being wrapped in the pastry.

BASIC CHOUX PASTE

150 ml ($\frac{1}{4}$ pint) water　　　　Pinch of salt
50 g (2 oz) butter　　　　　　　2 eggs
65 g (2$\frac{1}{2}$ oz) plain flour

Heat the water and butter in a medium saucepan until just boiling. Remove from the heat and stir in the flour and salt. As soon as the flour is absorbed, place over gentle heat and beat with a wooden spoon until the paste leaves the sides of the pan clean. Cool until bearable to the touch then add the eggs, one at a time, beating with a wooden spoon after each addition until smooth. Place in a piping bag fitted with a 1.25 cm ($\frac{1}{2}$ inch) plain nozzle. Force out the paste on to greased and floured baking sheets – into 7.5 cm (3 inch) lengths for eclairs or into balls the size of a walnut for puffs. Bake in a moderately hot oven (200°C, 400°F, Gas Mark 6) for 15–20 minutes, or until golden brown and crisp. Cut down the side of each eclair and across each puff without cutting through, to allow the steam to escape. Cool on a wire rack.

Makes about 12 eclairs or 24 choux puffs.

Eclairs – Fill with sweetened whipped cream and coat tops with chocolate icing – Blend 2 tablespoons boiling water into 3 tablespoons cocoa powder. When smooth gradually beat in 225 g (8 oz) sifted icing sugar. To make coffee icing, dissolve 1 teaspoon instant coffee in 2 tablespoons boiling water then gradually beat in the icing sugar as above.

Profiteroles – Fill the puffs with sweetened whipped cream, and carefully press together again. Serve piled up in a glass dish with a hot chocolate sauce poured over – Melt 75 g (3 oz) plain chocolate with 2 tablespoons golden syrup, 2 tablespoons water and 15 g ($\frac{1}{2}$ oz) butter in a small pan. Stir until smooth.

BASIC SUET PASTRY

225 g (8 oz) self-raising　　　　100 g (4 oz) shredded
　flour　　　　　　　　　　　　beef suet
Pinch of salt　　　　　　　　　About 150 ml ($\frac{1}{4}$ pint) cold
　　　　　　　　　　　　　　　　water

Sift the flour with the salt and stir in the suet. Add sufficient water to make a firm dough. Turn out on a lightly floured surface and knead lightly until smooth. Cover and leave to rest for 15 minutes before using.

This quantity is sufficient to line and cover a 1 litre (1$\frac{3}{4}$ pint) pudding basin or to make a baked roly poly to serve 6.

Yield: about 450 g (1 lb) pastry.

PORK AND LEEK PUDDING

450 g (1 lb) basic suet pastry*
350 g (12 oz) lean pork, diced
3 medium leeks, sliced

2 tablespoons seasoned flour
1 teaspoon dried sage
About 300 ml ($\frac{1}{2}$ pint) warm chicken stock

Roll out two-thirds of the pastry and use to line a 1 litre (1$\frac{3}{4}$ pint) pudding basin. Layer the pork and leek in the pudding case, sprinkling each layer with flour and sage. Pour in sufficient stock to come about three-quarters of the way up the pudding. Roll out the remaining pastry to make a lid, lift over the pudding, dampen the edges and seal well together. Cover with greased foil and crimp the edges securely under the rim of the basin. Stand it in a saucepan and pour in boiling water to come half-way up the sides of the basin. Cover the pan and boil for 3$\frac{1}{2}$ hours, adding more boiling water to the pan as necessary.
Serves 4.

Jam Roly-Poly − Roll out 450 g (1 lb) basic suet pastry to a rectangle 25 cm (10 inches) by 20 cm (8 inches). Spread over 5 tablespoons jam to within 2.5 cm (1 inch) of the edge. Fold in this border. Dampen the edges and roll up loosely starting from one short side, pressing edges to seal. Place, seal downwards, in a shallow ovenproof dish, slash the top lightly 3 times and bake in a moderately hot oven (190°C, 375°F, Gas Mark 5) for 40 minutes.

111

SIMPLE SAUSAGE ROLLS

*225 g (8 oz) frozen puff
 pastry, defrosted*

*8 chipolata sausages
Beaten egg to glaze*

Roll out the pastry to a rectangle 30 cm (12 inches) by 17.5 cm (7 inches) and divide in half down the long length. Lay 4 sausages, end to end, down the centre of each strip of pastry, brush the pastry edges with beaten egg, fold over the pastry to enclose the sausages and press the edges to seal. Cut each roll into 4 equal pieces and prick the tops once or twice. Place on a damped baking sheet, brush with beaten egg and bake in a hot oven (230°C, 450°F, Gas Mark 8) for about 20 minutes, until well risen and golden brown.
Makes 8.

VOL-AU-VENT CASES

*450 g (1 lb) frozen puff
 pastry, defrosted*

Beaten egg to glaze

Roll out the pastry to a thickness of 1.25 cm ($\frac{1}{2}$ inch) and stamp out eight 7.5 cm (3 inch) rounds with a fluted biscuit cutter. Place the rounds on a damped baking sheet and cut half-way through the pastry of each round with a plain 3.75 cm ($1\frac{1}{2}$ inch) biscuit cutter. Brush with beaten egg and bake in a hot oven (230°C, 450°F, Gas Mark 8) for 20 minutes, until well risen and browned. Ease out the pastry lids and press down the soft inside of each vol-au-vent case with the back of a teaspoon.
Makes 8.

Bouchées – Roll out the pastry to a thickness of 0.65 cm ($\frac{1}{4}$ inch), stamp into 5 cm (2 inch) rounds and use a 2.5 cm (1 inch) cutter to make the lids. Baking time will be about 15 minutes.

FRUIT ENVELOPES

350 g (12 oz) frozen puff
    pastry
175 g (6 oz) canned fruit
    pie filling

100 g (4 oz) chopped
    dessert apple
Beaten egg white to glaze
Castor sugar to sprinkle

Roll out the pastry to a rectangle 45 cm (18 inches) by 30 cm (12 inches) and divide into six 12 cm (6 inch) squares. Mix the pie filling with the apple, divide between the squares and brush all the pastry edges with beaten egg white. Bring all four corners of each square to the centre over the filling and press to seal well together. (Alternatively, fold one corner of each square across the filling and press to the opposite corner to make triangular turnovers.) Place the envelopes on a damped baking sheet, brush with egg white, sprinkle with castor sugar and bake in a moderately hot oven (200°C, 400°F, Gas Mark 6) for 20 minutes, until golden brown.

Makes 6.

(It is easier and more economical to make envelopes or triangular turnovers rather than the half-moon shapes where you must stamp circles out of the pastry, leaving many trimmings.)

Bread Making

BREAD LOAVES AND ROLLS

BASIC WHITE BREAD DOUGH

1 teaspoon sugar
900 ml (1½ pints) hand
  hot water
1 tablespoon dried
  yeast

1.5 kg (3 lb) strong
  white flour
4 teaspoons salt
50 g (2 oz) butter

Dissolve the sugar in the water and sprinkle the yeast on the liquid. Leave in a warm place for about 10 minutes, until frothy. Sift the flour and salt into a large warm mixing bowl and rub in the butter. Pour in the yeast liquid and mix to a dough which leaves the sides of the bowl clean. Turn out on a floured surface and knead for 10 minutes, until the dough is firm, elastic and no longer sticky. Return the dough to the bowl, cover with greased polythene and allow to rise in a warm place for about 1 hour, until double in bulk. (The lower the temperature, the longer the dough will take to rise.) Turn out on to a floured surface again and knead lightly until firm.

Yield: about 2.5 kg (5½ lb) risen dough.

Variations:

Brown Bread Dough – Substitute 0.75 kg (1½ lb) wholemeal flour for half the white flour.

Bran Bread – Substitute 225 g (8 oz) unprocessed natural bran for an equal weight of white flour. Increase the sugar to 2 teaspoons and the yeast to 4 teaspoons.

Large Tin Loaf – Take 1 kg (2 lb 3 oz) risen dough and shape to a large rectangle. Roll up from one short side and place in a greased 1 kg (2 lb) loaf tin, tucking the ends in neatly.

Large Plaited Loaf – Take 1 kg (2 lb 3 oz) risen dough and divide into 3 equal portions. Lay them side by side and plait them from the centre to each end. Place on a greased baking sheet, tucking the ends under neatly.

Small Bumpy Loaf – Take 500 g (18 oz) risen dough and divide into 5 equal portions. Shape each into a flat round and stack them one on top of each other. Fit the stack, on its side, into a greased 450 g (1 lb) loaf tin and press lightly.

Small Cottage Loaf – Take 500 g (18 oz) risen dough and pinch off one third. Shape each piece into a flat round and place the larger one on a greased baking sheet. Dampen the surface and put the smaller round on top. Flour the handle of a wooden spoon and push this down through the centre of both rounds of dough to touch the baking sheet.

Cloverleaf Rolls – Take 50 g (2 oz) risen dough and divide into 3 equal portions. Shape each into a ball and place the 3 balls together and just touching, on a greased baking sheet.

Knotted Rolls – Take 50 g (2 oz) risen dough and roll to a sausage shape about 15 cm (6 inches) long. Tie in a single knot and place on a greased baking sheet.

Coburg Rolls – Take 50 g (2 oz) risen dough and shape into a smooth ball. Place on a greased baking sheet and cut a deep cross in the top with a sharp knife.

Proving and Baking

Cover shaped loaves or rolls with greased polythene and leave in a warm place to prove. This will take from about 45 minutes for large or small loaves, whether in tins or on baking sheets, and about 30 minutes for rolls. The dough should either reach the top of the tin or almost double in size. Leave dough plain or brush with milk, beaten egg or melted butter. If liked, sprinkle with cracked wheat, poppy seeds or sesame seeds. Bake large loaves in a hot oven (230°C, 450°F, Gas Mark 8) for 20 minutes, then reduce heat to moderately hot (200°C, 400°F, Gas Mark 6) for a further 15–20 minutes. Bake small loaves in a hot oven (220°C, 425°F, Gas Mark 7) for 40–45 minutes and rolls in a hot oven (230°C, 450°F, Gas Mark 8) for 20 minutes. Baked bread should sound hollow when tapped on the base with the knuckles. After baking, cool on a wire rack.

TOMATO AND ANCHOVY PIZZA

1 medium onion, sliced
Little oil
225 g (8 oz) tomatoes
1 clove garlic, crushed
$\frac{1}{2}$ teaspoon dried mixed
  herbs
1 tablespoon tomato
  purée

$\frac{1}{2}$ teaspoon sugar
Salt and pepper
300 g (10 oz) risen white
  bread dough*
50 g (2 oz) can anchovy
  fillets
75 g (3 oz) Cheddar
  cheese, grated

Fry the onion gently in 2 tablespoons oil until soft. Chop the tomatoes and add to the pan with the garlic, herbs, tomato purée and sugar. Bring to the boil and cook for 10 minutes, or until thick. Season with salt and pepper. Roll out the dough to a 22.5 cm (9 inch) circle and place on a greased baking sheet. Brush lightly with oil. Spoon over the tomato mixture and make a lattice of anchovy fillets on top. Sprinkle with the cheese and drizzle over the anchovy oil. Bake in a hot oven (220°C, 425°F, Gas Mark 7) for about 30 minutes.

Serves 2–3.

Variation:

Mini Ham Pizzas – Divide 450 g (1 lb) risen white bread dough into 4 equal portions and roll each out to a 15 cm (6 inch) circle. Place on greased baking sheets and brush with oil. Slice 4 large tomatoes and arrange on the bases. Top with 175 g (6 oz) chopped ham and sprinkle over 100 g (4 oz) grated Gouda cheese. Bake in a moderately hot oven (190°C, 375°F, Gas Mark 5) for 25 minutes.

Serves 4.

FRUITIE BUNS

450 g (1 lb) risen white
  bread dough*
50 g (2 oz) sultanas
50 g (2 oz) glacé
  cherries, chopped

50 g (2 oz) chopped
  mixed peel
3 tablespoons clear honey

Place the dough in a mixing bowl and gradually work in the fruit, peel and 2 tablespoons honey. Divide into 8 equal portions and shape each into a round ball. Place on a greased baking sheet, with space between them. Cover with greased polythene and allow to prove in a warm place for about 30 minutes, until almost double in size. Bake in a moderately hot oven (190°C, 375°F, Gas Mark 5) for 15–20 minutes, until golden brown. Brush the tops of the hot buns with the remaining honey to glaze them. Cool on a wire rack.
Makes 8.

APRICOT AND WALNUT TEABREAD

75 g (3 oz) dried apricots	2 tablespoons milk
75 g (3 oz) soft margarine	350 g (12 oz) self-raising flour, sifted
2 tablespoons golden syrup	50 g (2 oz) chopped walnuts
75 g (3 oz) soft brown sugar	3 eggs

Soak the apricots in cold water overnight. Drain and chop. Place the margarine, syrup, sugar and milk in a pan and heat gently, stirring, until the sugar has dissolved. Cool until lukewarm. Place the flour and nuts in a mixing bowl, drop in the eggs and beat, gradually drawing in the flour and adding the syrup mixture little by little. Beat just long enough to incorporate all the flour then stir in the apricots and turn into a greased 1 kg (2 lb) loaf tin. Bake in a moderate oven (160°C, 325°F, Gas Mark 3) for about $1\frac{1}{4}$ hours, until firm to the touch. Cool on a wire rack. Serve sliced with butter.
Makes 1 1 kg (2 lb) loaf.

BANANA BREAD

100 g (4 oz) butter or margarine	1 tablespoon baking powder
100 g (4 oz) soft brown	$\frac{1}{2}$ teaspoon salt

sugar   Pinch of ground nutmeg
1 egg, beaten   3 ripe bananas
225 g (8 oz) plain flour

Cream the butter and sugar until light and fluffy, then gradually
beat in the egg. Sift the flour, baking powder, salt and nutmeg
together. Mash the bananas and add to the creamed mixture
alternately with the dry ingredients. Mix well, turn into a well-
greased 1 kg (2 lb) loaf tin and bake in a moderate oven (180°C,
350°F, Gas Mark 4) for about 1 hour, or until a fine skewer
inserted in the centre comes out clean. Cool on a wire rack.
Serve sliced with butter.
Makes 1 1 kg (2 lb) loaf.
Variation:
Fruited Banana Bread – Add 100 g (4 oz) sultanas with the
flour mixture and sprinkle the surface with 25 g (1 oz) chopped
mixed nuts before baking.

Cakes and Biscuits

BASIC VANILLA ALL-IN-ONE CAKE MIXTURE

100 g (4 oz) self-raising
 flour
1 teaspoon baking powder
100 g (4 oz) soft
 margarine

100 g (4 oz) castor
 sugar
2 eggs
½ teaspoon vanilla
 essence

Sift the flour with the baking powder into a bowl and add the remaining ingredients. Beat with a wooden spoon for 2–3 minutes, until the mixture is smooth and well blended. Sufficient for 2 17.5 cm (7 inch) layers, 18 small cakes or 16 finger cakes.

Variations:
Lemon Cake Mixture – Add the grated rind of 1 lemon and omit the vanilla essence.
Chocolate Cake Mixture – Blend 2 tablespoons cocoa powder with 2 tablespoons hot water. Cool and add to the bowl when mixing.
Jam Sandwich Cake – Divide 1 quantity of Vanilla Cake Mixture* between two greased and base-lined 17.5 cm (7 inch) sandwich tins. Bake in a moderate oven (160°C, 325°F, Gas Mark 3) for about 30 minutes, until firm to the touch. Cool on a wire rack and sandwich together with raspberry jam. Sift the top with icing sugar.
Lemon Cup Cakes – Divide 1 quantity of Lemon Cake Mixture* between 18 paper bun cases and bake in a moderately hot oven (190°C, 375°F, Gas Mark 5) for about 15 minutes, until golden brown. When cold cover with lemon glacé icing – sift 225 g (8 oz) icing sugar and gradually work in 1 tablespoon warm water and 1–2 tablespoons lemon juice, until creamy.
Mocha Bars – Spread 1 quantity Chocolate Cake Mixture* in a greased and base-lined swiss roll tin. Bake in a moderately hot

oven (200°C, 400°F, Gas Mark 6) for about 12 minutes, until golden brown. Cool and spread with coffee butter cream − Dissolve 1 teaspoon instant coffee in 1 tablespoon boiling water. Cool and combine with 100 g (4 oz) butter and 225 g (8 oz) sifted icing sugar. Cut the cake into 16 fingers.

EVERYDAY FRUIT CAKE

225 g (8 oz) plain flour
1 teaspoon baking powder
1 teaspoon ground mixed
   spice
Grated rind of $\frac{1}{2}$ orange
300 g (10 oz) mixed
   dried fruit

50 g (2 oz) chopped
   mixed peel
2 tablespoons milk
150 g (5 oz) castor sugar
2 eggs
150 g (5 oz) butter or
   margarine

Place all the ingredients in a mixing bowl and beat with a wooden spoon for about 3 minutes, until well blended. Turn into a greased and lined 17.5 cm (7 inch) cake tin and bake in a cool oven (150°C, 300°F, Gas Mark 2) for about $1\frac{3}{4}$ hours, or until a fine skewer inserted in the centre comes out clean. Leave in the tin for 5 minutes then turn out on a wire rack, strip off the lining paper and cool.
Makes 1 17.5 cm (7 inch) cake.

RICH FRUIT CAKE

325 g (11 oz) plain flour
$\frac{1}{2}$ teaspoon baking powder
2 teaspoons ground mixed
   spice
Grated rind of 1 small
   orange
0.75 kg ($1\frac{1}{2}$ lb) mixed
   dried fruit
75 g (3 oz) chopped
   mixed peel

50 g (2 oz) glacé
   cherries, chopped
2 tablespoons milk
225 g (8 oz) castor
   sugar
5 eggs
225 g (8 oz) butter or
   margarine

Make the cake mixture as above and bake in a greased and lined

20 cm (8 inch) cake tin for about $3\frac{3}{4}$ hours. Leave in the tin for 15 minutes before turning out.

Makes 1 20 cm (8 inch) cake.

DARK RICH FRUIT CAKE

275 g (9 oz) plain flour
2 teaspoons ground
  mixed spice
Grated rind of 1 orange
1 kg (2 lb) mixed dried
  fruit
100 g (4 oz) chopped
  mixed peel
100 g (4 oz) glacé
  cherries, halved
2 tablespoons brandy
  or sherry

1 tablespoon black
  treacle
225 g (8 oz) soft brown
  sugar
6 eggs
225 g (8 oz) butter or
  margarine
50 g (2 oz) ground
  almonds
50 g (2 oz) chopped
  almonds

Make the cake mixture as above and turn into a greased and lined 22.5 cm (9 inch) cake tin. Tie a double thickness of brown paper round the outside of the tin, to extend 5 cm (2 inches) above the top of the tin. Bake in the oven as above for $1\frac{1}{2}$ hours then reduce the heat to very cool (120°C, 250°F, Gas Mark $\frac{1}{2}$) and cook for about a further 3 hours. Cover the cake with a sheet of foil after the first $2\frac{1}{2}$ hours to prevent over browning. Leave in the tin for 15 minutes before turning out. Store in an airtight tin for 1 month before eating.

Makes 1 22.5 cm (9 inch) cake.

STICKY GINGERBREAD

450 g (1 lb) plain flour
1 tablespoon ground
  ginger
1 tablespoon baking
  powder
1 teaspoon bicarbonate
  of soda
1 teaspoon salt
175 g (6 oz) margarine

175 g (6 oz) black
  treacle
175 g (6 oz) golden
  syrup
225 g (8 oz) demerara
  sugar
300 ml ($\frac{1}{2}$ pint) milk
1 egg, beaten

Sift the flour, ginger, baking powder, bicarbonate of soda and salt together into a mixing bowl. Place the margarine, treacle, syrup and sugar in a saucepan and heat gently just until the fat melts. Remove from the heat and stir in the milk and egg. Pour into the dry ingredients and beat well until the batter is smooth. Turn into a greased and lined 20 cm (8 inch) square cake tin and bake in a moderate oven (180°C, 350°F, Gas Mark 4) for about $1\frac{1}{2}$ hours, or until well risen and just firm to the touch. Leave in the tin for 20 minutes then turn out on a wire rack and carefully remove the lining paper. When cold, store in an airtight tin for at least 24 hours before cutting.

Makes 1 large cake, 9 squares.

PLAIN TEA SCONES

225 g (8 oz) self-raising
*   flour*
$\frac{1}{2}$ teaspoon salt
50 g (2 oz) soft
*   margarine*

25 g (1 oz) castor sugar
About 150 ml ($\frac{1}{4}$ pint)
*   milk*

Sift the flour and salt into a bowl and rub in the fat until the mixture resembles fine breadcrumbs. Stir in the sugar and add sufficient milk to make a soft but not sticky dough. Turn out on a floured surface and pat out to a thickness of about 2 cm ($\frac{3}{4}$ inch) and cut into rounds with a 5 cm (2 inch) cutter. Transfer to a greased baking sheet and brush with milk. Bake in a hot oven (220°C, 425°F, Gas Mark 7) for 8–10 minutes, until well risen and golden brown. Serve warm.

Makes about 12.

Variations:

Fruit Scones – Add 25 g (1 oz) currants, sultanas or finely chopped dates with the sugar before mixing.

Cheese Scones – Omit the sugar and add a pinch of cayenne pepper with the salt. Stir in 50 g (2 oz) finely grated Cheddar after the fat is added. Brush the scones with beaten egg before baking.

WHEATGERM DROP SCONES

75 g (3 oz) wholemeal
   flour
25 g (1 oz) wheatgerm
$\frac{1}{2}$ teaspoon bicarbonate
   of soda
Pinch of salt

1 teaspoon cream of
   tartar
1 egg
150 ml ($\frac{1}{4}$ pint) milk
2 tablespoons oil
Little extra oil for
   cooking

Mix the flour thoroughly with the wheatgerm, bicarbonate of soda, salt and cream of tartar in a mixing bowl. Beat the egg with the milk and oil and pour into the bowl. Whisk, gradually drawing in the dry ingredients, until the batter is smooth. Heat a griddle or heavy frying pan and brush lightly with oil. Using a tablespoon of mixture for each scone, pour the batter into the pan from the tip of the spoon, to give neat round scones. Cook over moderate heat until the tops are covered with bubbles, then turn with a palette knife and brown the other sides. Stack up the scones on a plate, cover with a clean teacloth to keep them soft and warm while you cook the rest of the batter. Serve the scones warm with butter.
Makes 16.

SHORTBREAD

100 g (4 oz) butter,
   softened
50 g (2 oz) castor sugar

150 g (5 oz) plain flour
25 g (1 oz) ground rice
Little extra castor sugar

Cream the butter and sugar together until light and fluffy. Sift the flour and, using a fork, gradually stir it into the butter mixture with the ground rice. Gather the mixture together with the fingertips and knead lightly until smooth. Press into a lightly buttered 17.5 cm (7 inch) sandwich tin. Prick all over with a fork and pinch the edges decoratively, with finger and thumb. Bake in a moderate oven (160°C, 325°F, Gas Mark 3) for about 40 minutes, or until pale straw in colour. Leave in the tin for 5 minutes then cut into 8 portions while still soft. When firm, transfer to a wire rack to cool. Sprinkle with sugar before serving.

Makes 8 pieces.

Variation:

Gingered Shortbread Fingers − Sift $\frac{1}{2}$ teaspoon ground ginger with the flour when mixing, press into a 15–17.5 cm (6–7 inch) buttered square tin and cut into 8 fingers after baking. Sprinkle with a little chopped crystallised or preserved ginger before serving, if wished.

FLAPJACK BARS

100 g (4 oz) butter or margarine	*75 g (3 oz) golden syrup*
	175 g (6 oz) rolled oats
100 g (4 oz) soft brown sugar	*50 g (2 oz) plain flour*

Put the butter, sugar and golden syrup into a saucepan and stir over a low heat until melted. Add the rolled oats and flour and mix well. Spread in a greased Swiss roll tin and bake in a moderate oven (180°C, 350°F, Gas Mark 4) for about 20 minutes, or until golden. Cool for 5 minutes then cut into 20 bars. Remove from the tin when cold.

Makes 20 bars.

SPICED COCONUT CRUNCHIES

75 g (3 oz) plain flour	*25 g (1 oz) desiccated coconut*
1 teaspoon ground cinnamon	
50 g (2 oz) semolina	*100 g (4 oz) soft margarine*
	50 g (2 oz) castor sugar

Sift the flour and cinnamon together and stir in the semolina and coconut. Cream the margarine with the sugar until light and fluffy, stir in the dry ingredients and mix well. Gather the mixture together and knead lightly until smooth. Pinch off

130

pieces of dough, each about the size of a small walnut, and arrange well apart on greased baking sheets. Bake in a moderate oven (160°C, 325°F, Gas Mark 3) for about 10 minutes, or until pale golden brown. Leave on the tins for 2 minutes, then lift on to a wire rack to cool.

Makes about 24.

Variation:

Almond Crisps − Substitute 25 g (1 oz) ground almonds for the coconut and use $\frac{1}{2}$ teaspoon almond essence instead of the cinnamon. Make up the dough and form into a roll about 5 cm (2 inches) in diameter. Wrap in cling film or foil and chill until really firm. Cut slices from the roll, each between 3−6 cm ($\frac{1}{8}$ − $\frac{1}{4}$ inch) thick, and arrange well apart on greased baking sheets. Top each biscuit with a piece of flaked almond and bake as above.

MERINGUES À LA CRÈME

2 egg whites	*Little extra sugar*
100 g (4 oz) castor	*150 ml ($\frac{1}{4}$ pint)*
sugar	*whipped cream*

Place the egg whites in a grease-free bowl and whisk until stiff. Gradually whisk in the sugar, a tablespoon at a time, until the meringue is firm and glossy. Using 2 dessert spoons to help you, shape the meringue into 12 shells on a baking sheet lined with non-stick cooking parchment. Alternatively, put the meringue into a piping bag fitted with a 1.25 cm ($\frac{1}{2}$ inch) nozzle and pipe out on the parchment. Sprinkle the shaped meringues lightly with castor sugar and place in a very cool oven (110°C, 225°F, Gas Mark $\frac{1}{4}$) for about 2 hours, until dry but still white. Cool on a wire rack. Put the meringue shells together in pairs with a filling of whipped cream.

Makes 6.

If you lack the patience to make these white meringues successfully, try this golden brown version using soft brown sugar.

Brown Sugar Meringue Cake − Whisk 2 egg whites with a pinch

131

of cream of tartar until stiff and gradually whisk in 100 g (4 oz) soft brown sugar, a tablespoon at a time, until the meringue is firm and glossy. Divide between two baking sheets lined with non-stick cooking parchment and spread each into a 20 cm (8 inch) round. Bake in a moderately hot oven (190°C, 375°F, Gas Mark 5) for 45 minutes. Cool on a wire rack and sandwich the meringue layers together with whipped cream or with a packet of instant dessert mix made up with half the required quantity of milk.

Variation:

Meringues Chantilly: Put the meringue halves together with vanilla icecream and pipe over the join with sweetened whipped cream. Finish with a glacé cherry.

CRUNCHY FLAN CASE

25 g (1 oz) butter or margarine	1 tablespoon cocoa
3 tablespoons golden syrup	1 tablespoon castor sugar
	75 g (3 oz) rice krispies

Place the butter, syrup, cocoa and sugar in a medium pan and bring to the boil, stirring constantly. Simmer for 1 minute then stir in the rice krispies. Press the mixture into a greased 20 cm (8 inch) flan dish or sandwich tin using the back of a tablespoon. Chill until firm before adding the chosen filling.

Serves 4.

Fillings:

Banana and Ice Cream – Slice 2 bananas and arrange in the flan case. Cover with scoops of firmly frozen vanilla ice cream arranged decoratively to cover the banana. Serve immediately.

Summer Fruit Fluff – Make up a packet of whipped dessert mix using only half the specified quantity of milk. Fold in 225 g (8 oz) sliced strawberries, raspberries or stoned cherries. Turn into the flan case and serve.

Simple Fluffy Filling – Make up the whipped dessert mix as above, spread in the flan case and sprinkle the surface with desiccated coconut before serving.

Desserts

STEAMED LEMON CURD PUDDING

3 tablespoons lemon
  curd

1 quantity Lemon
  all-in-one cake mixture*

Place the lemon curd in the base of a greased 900 ml (1½ pint) pudding basin. Spoon in the cake mixture and cover the basin securely with greased and pleated foil. Stand in a pan and add boiling water to come half-way up the sides of the basin. Keep the water boiling gently, cover the pan and cook for about 1½ hours, until the pudding is well risen and firm to the touch. Add more boiling water to the pan as necessary during cooking. Turn out and serve hot.

Serves 4.

Variation:

Steamed Tutti-Frutti Pudding – Omit the lemon curd. Drain and chop 1 ring of canned pineapple and chop 25 g (1 oz) glacé cherries. Stir these into the cake mixture with 25 g (1 oz) sultanas and turn into the greased pudding basin. Steam as above.

EVE'S FRUIT PUDDING

450 g (1 lb) prepared
  fruit such as cooking
  apple slices,
  blackberries, goose-
  berries, apricots,
  plums, cherries

About 100 g (4 oz)
  castor sugar
1 quantity Vanilla
  all-in-one cake
  mixture*

Layer the chosen fruit (or any combination) in a greased 1.5 litre (2½ pint) ovenproof pie dish, sprinkling each layer with sugar. Spread over the cake mixture and bake in a moderate oven

(180°C, 350°F, Gas Mark 4) for 1–1¼ hours, or until a fine skewer inserted in the centre of the topping comes out clean and the surface is golden brown. Sprinkle with a little more sugar and serve hot with cream or custard.

Serves 4.

Variation:

Gingered Rhubarb Pudding – Chop 2 pieces of preserved ginger and mix with 450 g (1 lb) thinly sliced rhubarb. Layer in the dish with sugar as above. Beat ½ teaspoon ground ginger into the cake mixture before spreading it over the fruit.

PLUM CRUMBLE

0.75 kg (1 ½ lb) plums
Castor sugar
75 g (3 oz) butter or
  margarine

175 g (6 oz) plain
  flour
¼ teaspoon ground
  cinnamon

Halve and stone the plums and place in a greased ovenproof dish. Sprinkle the fruit lightly with sugar if it is very tart. Rub the fat into the flour until the mixture resembles breadcrumbs. Stir in 75 g (3 oz) sugar and the cinnamon, and sprinkle over the fruit. Bake in a moderately hot oven (200°C, 400°F, Gas Mark 6) for about 30–35 minutes, until the top is golden brown. Alternatively, the crumble will cook just as well in a moderate oven if you are using the oven at this heat, but allow 40–45 minutes baking time. Serve hot with custard or ice cream.

Serves 4–6.

DANISH LAYERED APPLE AND CRUMB DESSERT

0.75 kg (1 ½ lb) cooking
  apples, peeled
4 tablespoons water
½ teaspoon ground
  cinnamon
2 tablespoons lemon
  marmalade
Castor sugar

100 g (4 oz) butter
175 g (6 oz) fresh
  white breadcrumbs
4 tablespoons demerara
  sugar
150 ml (¼ pint) double
  cream, whipped

Core and slice the apples into a pan. Pour over the water and cook gently for about 10 minutes until the apple is soft. Beat until smooth, with the cinnamon and marmalade, and sweeten to taste with castor sugar. Allow to cool. Melt the butter and use to fry the breadcrumbs, stirring frequently, until golden brown and crisp. Stir in the demerara sugar, remove from the heat and allow to cool. Put one third of the apple in the base of a glass serving dish and spoon over evenly one third of the buttered crumbs. Repeat these layers twice. Spread the cream over the surface before serving.

Serves 4–6.

Variation:

Snowflake Apple Dessert – Omit the cream and cover the surface with 75 g (3 oz) plain chocolate curls, made by scraping a potato peeler across the flat surface of a block of chocolate. Sift 1 tablespoon icing sugar through a fine strainer over the top to resemble snow.

RICH LEMON CHEESECAKE

100 g (4 oz) digestive
  biscuits, crushed
25 g (1 oz) soft brown
  sugar
50 g (2 oz) butter,
  melted
175 g (6 oz) full fat
  cream cheese
175 g (6 oz) cottage
  cheese, sieved

75 g (3 oz) castor sugar
Grated rind of 1 lemon
Juice of 2 lemons
15 g ($\frac{1}{2}$ oz) gelatine
2 tablespoons cold water
150 ml ($\frac{1}{4}$ pint)
  whipping cream

Mix together the biscuit crumbs, brown sugar and butter. Press to the base and sides of a buttered 17.5 cm (7 inch) loose-bottomed cake or flan tin, using the back of a metal spoon. Chill while preparing the filling. Beat together the cheeses, sugar and lemon rind and juice until smooth. Dissolve the gelatine in the water in a small basin over a pan of hot water. Beat into the cheese mixture. Whip the cream until thick, fold in lightly and turn into the prepared tin. Chill until set then ease off the tin and serve the cheesecake on the metal base.

Serves 4–6.

Variations:

Celebration Lemon Cheesecake – For an even richer cheesecake use chocolate digestive biscuits for the base and all cream cheese to make the filling, instead of half and half cream cheese and cottage cheese. Decorate with chocolate curls before serving.

Pineapple Cheesecake – Substitute 100 g (4 oz) drained crushed pineapple for the lemon juice and rind. Reduce the castor sugar to 50 g (2 oz).

AMERICAN CHEESECAKE

100 g (4 oz) digestive biscuits

$\frac{1}{2}$ teaspoon ground cinnamon

40 g (1$\frac{1}{2}$ oz) butter, melted

450 g (1 lb) cottage cheese, sieved

175 g (6 oz) castor sugar

3 tablespoons double cream

3 eggs

25 g (1 oz) flour, sifted

1 teaspoon grated orange rind

$\frac{1}{2}$ teaspoon grated lemon rind

Crush the biscuits and mix with the cinnamon and melted butter. Spread the mixture evenly over the base of a buttered 17.5 cm (7 inch) loose-bottomed round cake or flan tin. Beat the cottage cheese until very smooth and gradually add the sugar, cream and eggs. Mix in the flour and the orange and lemon rinds. Blend thoroughly and pour into the prepared tin. Bake in a cool oven (150°C, 300°F, Gas Mark 2) for 1$\frac{1}{4}$ hours, or until set. Turn off the heat, open the oven door slightly and leave the cheesecake in the oven for a further 30 minutes. Carefully remove from the tin when quite cold.

Serves 4–6.

Variation:

Cheesecake Tart – Line the flan tin with 175 g (6 oz) rich short-crust pastry, pour in the filling and bake in a moderate oven

(180°C, 350°F, Gas Mark 4) for 10 minutes, then reduce the heat to (150°C, 300°F, Gas Mark 2) and bake for a further 1 hour, or until the filling is set. Finish cooking as above.

TRADITIONAL TRIFLE

1 packet trifle sponges
4 tablespoons raspberry
    jam
425 g (15 oz) can peach
    slices
4 tablespoons sweet
    sherry

1 large banana
600 ml (1 pint) vanilla-
    flavoured custard
150 ml ($\frac{1}{4}$ pint) double
    cream, whipped
25 g (1 oz) toasted
    flaked almonds

Split the trifle sponges and spread with jam. Arrange in the base of a large glass dish and pour over the syrup from the can of peaches and the sherry. Leave to soak for at least 20 minutes then slice the banana over the top, cover with the peach slices and pour over the custard. When set, pipe or spread the cream over the surface and spike with the toasted almonds.
Serves 4–6.

APRICOT FOOL

450 g (1 lb) apricots
4 tablespoons water
Sugar

150 ml ($\frac{1}{4}$ pint) cold
    sweetened custard
150 ml ($\frac{1}{4}$ pint) double
    cream, whipped

Halve and stone the apricots and place in a saucepan with the water and 2 tablespoons sugar. Cook gently until the fruit is soft. Drain off and reserve the syrup. Sieve or liquidise the fruit, measure the purée and make up to 450 ml ($\frac{3}{4}$ pint) with reserved syrup. Taste and add extra sugar if necessary. When cold, mix together the fruit purée and custard and fold in the cream. Turn into a glass dish and serve with sponge fingers.
Serves 4–6.

RICH ORANGE MOUSSE

2 eggs
1 egg yolk
75 g (3 oz) castor sugar
15 g (½ oz) gelatine
3 tablespoons water

150 ml (¼ pint)
defrosted concentrated
orange juice
150 ml (¼ pint) double
cream, whipped

Whisk the eggs, egg yolk and sugar together until really thick. The mixture is ready when it falls from the whisk in a spiral and holds its shape. Dissolve the gelatine in the water in a basin over a pan of hot water. Whisk the dissolved gelatine into the egg mixture with the orange juice. Fold in the cream and turn immediately into a glass serving dish. Chill until set and serve plain.
Serves 4–6.

GOOSEBERRY CREAM

Water
Sugar
450 g (1 lb) gooseberries
15 g (½ oz) gelatine

Few drops green food
colouring
300 ml (½ pint)
whipping cream

Place 300 ml (½ pint) water in a saucepan with 50 g (2 oz) sugar and the gooseberries. Poach the fruit for about 15 minutes, until soft. Drain and reserve the syrup. Rub the fruit through a sieve to remove the seeds and skins and measure the purée. Make it up to 450 ml (¾ pint) with reserved syrup. Dissolve the gelatine in a further 3 tablespoons of the reserved syrup then stir into the purée and tint pale green with a few drops of food colour. Check and add more sugar if wished. When the mixture begins to thicken, whip the cream and fold it in evenly until blended. Turn into a glass dish and chill until set.
Serves 4–6.
Variation:
Strawberry Creams – Reserve 6 good strawberries from 450 g (1 lb) and press the remainder through a sieve. Sweeten the purée to taste and make up to 450 ml (¾ pint) with orange juice if

necessary. Use instead of the gooseberry purée. Dissolve the gelatine in a further 3 tablespoons of orange juice and continue as above. Divide between 6 wine glasses and when set decorate each cream with a strawberry.

JELLIES

Take advantage of the many differently flavoured jellies available today to make attractive sweets easily.

Whisked Jelly Mousse
Chill a large can of evaporated milk. Make up a fruit jelly with 150 ml ($\frac{1}{4}$ pint) boiling water then allow to cool. Whisk the milk with an electric mixer or by hand until thick then gradually whisk in the cooled jelly. Turn into a glass dish and leave to set.

Marshmallow Jelly
Make up a fruit jelly with 300 ml ($\frac{1}{2}$ pint) boiling water and when dissolved stir in 75 g (3 oz) marshmallows, until they melt and the mixture is quite smooth. Turn into a rinsed jelly mould and chill until set. Turn out to serve.

Fruit Jelly
Drain the syrup from a 425 g (15 oz) can of fruit cocktail or other fruit. Make up the syrup to 450 ml ($\frac{3}{4}$ pint) with water, bring to the boil and use to dissolve a fruit jelly. Leave to cool then stir in the fruit and turn into a rinsed jelly mould. Turn out to serve.

Any of these desserts can be topped with whipped cream when set to give them a festive look.

CHOCOLATE BAKED ALASKA

1 layer baked chocolate sponge	2 egg white quantity basic meringue*
3 tablespoons Cointreau	0.5 litre (17.5 fl oz) chocolate ice cream

Place the chocolate sponge on an ovenproof dish and sprinkle over the Cointreau (or use orange juice if you wish). Make the meringue. Using a sharp knife, cut up the ice cream and arrange the pieces, close together, in a domed shape on top of the sponge. Cover completely with meringue, right down to the dish, and swirl the outside with the blade of a knife. Place in a hot oven (220°C, 425°F, Gas Mark 7) for 4–5 minutes, or until the meringue is golden brown. Serve at once.
Serves 4.

Egg and Cheese Dishes

CHEESE PUDDING

4 large slices stale
  bread
Butter for spreading
225 g (8 oz) Cheddar
  cheese, grated

Pinch of cayenne pepper
600 ml (1 pint) milk
1 egg

Remove the crusts from the bread and toast the slices on one side only. Butter the untoasted side of each. Put 2 slices of toast, buttered side upwards, in a greased ovenproof dish, sprinkle with half the cheese, season with the cayenne pepper and cover with the remaining slices of bread, toasted side upwards. Sprinkle over the rest of the cheese. Heat the milk to boiling point, cool slightly and whisk in the egg. Pour over the ingredients in the dish and allow to stand for at least 30 minutes. Bake in a moderately hot oven (200°C, 400°F, Gas Mark 6) for 20 minutes, or until puffed up and golden brown.
Serves 4.

GOUGÈRE

1 quantity basic choux
  paste*
150 g (5 oz) strong
  Cheddar cheese, grated
$\frac{1}{4}$ teaspoon pepper

450 g (1 lb) cooked meat
150 ml ($\frac{1}{4}$ pint) thick
  brown gravy
1 tablespoon tomato
  ketchup

Make up the choux paste, beat in 75 g (3 oz) of the cheese and the pepper and spoon the mixture round the edge of a greased shallow ovenproof dish. Finely chop the meat, moisten with gravy and stir in the ketchup. Put the meat mixture in the centre of the dish and fork a little of the choux paste over it. Sprinkle

with the remaining cheese and bake in a moderately hot oven (200°C, 400°F, Gas Mark 6) for 35–40 minutes, or until well risen and golden brown. Serve hot with a mixed salad.
Serves 4.

Variation:

Fish Gougère – Substitute 450 g (1 lb) cooked flaked white fish for the meat and use 150 ml ($\frac{1}{4}$ pint) basic white sauce* instead of the gravy and ketchup.

POTTED LANCASHIRE CHEESE

450 g (1 lb) fresh
   Lancashire cheese
7 tablespoons dry sherry

7 tablespoons double
   cream
Salt and pepper
Melted butter

Grate or crumble the cheese and place in a pan with the sherry and cream. Season to taste with salt and pepper and place over gentle heat, stirring all the time until the cheese melts and the mixture is smooth. Pour into small pots and allow to cool. Cover the surface of each pot with a little melted butter and store in the refrigerator. Use within 1 month.
Serves 4.

Variation:

Herbed Potted Cheese – Stir 3 tablespoons finely chopped parsley or chives into the cheese mixture while it is heating.

DUTCH FONDUE

1 clove garlic
150 ml ($\frac{1}{4}$ pint) dry
   white wine
1 teaspoon lemon juice
450 g (1 lb) Gouda
   cheese, grated

1 tablespoon cornflour
2 tablespoons gin
Black pepper
Ground nutmeg
1 large French loaf,
   cubed

Rub the inside of a thick-based shallow pan with garlic and place a little finely chopped garlic in the pan. Pour in the wine and

lemon juice, bring to the boil then reduce the heat to simmering point and gradually add the cheese, stirring continuously with a wooden spoon, until it melts. Bring to the boil again. Meanwhile, blend the cornflour with the gin until smooth, add to the cheese mixture and stir well. Season with black pepper and nutmeg to taste and serve immediately with the bread.
Serves 4.

STUFFED EGGS MORNAY

6 eggs, hard-boiled
$\frac{1}{2}$ small onion
100 g (4 oz) mushrooms
15 g ($\frac{1}{2}$ oz) butter
1 tablespoon oil
2 teaspoons tomato
  purée
Pinch of sugar

1 teaspoon chopped
  parsley
Salt and pepper
300 ml ($\frac{1}{2}$ pint) whisked
  cheese sauce*
50 g (2 oz) Cheddar
  cheese, grated

Halve the eggs lengthways and remove the yolks. Finely chop the onion and mushrooms. Heat the butter and oil in a small pan and use to fry the onion gently until soft but not brown. Stir in the mushrooms and cook briskly for a further 3 minutes. Mix in the tomato purée, sugar, parsley and seasoning to taste. Mash the egg yolks into the mixture and use to fill the egg white halves. Arrange them in a shallow ovenproof dish, spoon over the sauce to cover them and sprinkle with the cheese. Cook in a hot oven (220°C, 425°F, Gas Mark 7) for about 15 minutes, or until golden brown on top.
Serves 4.

RUSSIAN STUFFED EGGS

100 g (4 oz) drained
  black olives
1 small onion, grated
$\frac{1}{2}$ teaspoon anchovy
  essence
2 tablespoons oil

1 teaspoon vinegar
Pinch of ground black
  pepper
4 eggs, hard-boiled
Shredded lettuce

147

Rinse the olives, stone them and chop finely. Place in a small bowl with the onion. Put the anchovy essence, oil, vinegar and pepper in a screw-topped jar and shake well until the dressing emulsifies. Pour it over the olive mixture and stir well. Halve the eggs and arrange them cut side upwards on a bed of shredded lettuce. Top each egg half with a rounded mound of the olive mixture.
Serves 4.

BASIC SCRAMBLED EGG

4 eggs	2 tablespoons milk or
Salt and pepper	cream
25 g (1 oz) butter	Hot buttered toast or
	fried bread

Beat the eggs with a fork until well blended and season with salt and pepper. Melt the butter in a saucepan over medium heat, pour in the egg mixture and cook, stirring with a metal spoon as the egg begins to set. Mix in the milk or cream and continue stirring until only a little of the egg is still liquid. Remove from the heat and stir until the mixture is evenly creamy. Serve immediately on hot buttered toast or with crisply fried bread.
Serves 2.

PIPÉRADE

Ingredients for basic	1 small sweet green or
scrambled egg*	red pepper, deseeded
1 small onion	1 large tomato, peeled

Melt the butter in a saucepan. Finely chop the onion and chop the pepper. Add to the pan and cook gently until soft, but not brown. Chop the tomato, stir into the onion mixture and cook for a further 3 minutes. Pour in the egg mixture and cook, stirring, until the egg is lightly scrambled. Serve immediately with crusty French bread and a green salad.
Serves 2–3.

PLAIN OMELETTE

2 *eggs*   *Salt and pepper*
2 *teaspoons cold water*   *15 g ($\frac{1}{2}$ oz) butter*

Break the eggs into a bowl, add the water and seasoning to taste and beat lightly with a fork. Heat a small pan gently while beating the eggs, put in the butter and increase the heat until it melts and sizzles. Pour in the egg mixture and cook for about 15 seconds, then stir gently with a fork and start drawing in the cooked egg from the sides of the pan, allowing any raw egg to run down on to the hot pan. When the underside is set and just turning golden and the top is still creamy, tilt the pan and fold the omelette in half, then slip it on to a warm plate.
Serves 1.

Savoury Fillings:
Add one of the following to the beaten eggs before cooking
  – Chopped chives, parsley, tarragon leaves or a mixture of
  these herbs.
Grated cheese, chopped ham or flaked cooked fish.

Sweet Fillings:
Omit the salt and pepper in the basic egg mixture and add 2
  teaspoons castor sugar and a little grated orange or lemon
  rind.
Cook the omelette and serve plain or fill with one of the
  following and sprinkle with icing sugar before serving –
Warmed jam, marmalade or puréed stewed fruit.
Chopped canned pineapple soaked in a little Kirsch.
Ice cream.

PANCAKES

The basic recipe which follows can be adapted in various ways, sweet as well as savoury. One quantity Crab Meat sauce* can be used as a savoury filling instead of the Bolognese sauce*. Canned cherry or apricot pie filling makes a delicious sweet stuffing for pancakes. Or the cooked pancakes can be spread with a mixture of butter, sugar and grated lemon or orange rind and served folded in four with orange or lemon wedges.

STUFFED PANCAKES

BATTER:

100 g (4 oz) plain flour	$\frac{1}{2}$ quantity hot
Pinch of salt	all-purpose
1 egg	Bolognese sauce*
2 tablespoons oil	100 g (4 oz) Cheddar
300 ml ($\frac{1}{2}$ pint) milk	cheese, grated
Little oil for frying	

Sift the flour and salt into a bowl, add the egg, oil and half the milk and whisk until smooth. Gradually beat in the remaining milk. Heat a small frying pan and brush lightly with oil. Make 8 thin pancakes, using about 3 tablespoons of batter for each one, cooking them until golden brown on each side and re-greasing the pan as necessary. Stack the cooked pancakes on a plate while you cook the rest of the batter. Divide the meat sauce between the 8 pancakes and roll each one up. Place them side by side in a shallow ovenproof dish and sprinkle evenly with the cheese. Place in a moderate oven (180°C, 350°F, Gas Mark 4) for 25 minutes, or until piping hot and golden brown on top. Serves 4.

CHEESE-BOARD PRESENTATION

A simple cheese-board can be made up using our own home-produced varieties. Two hard cheeses, one mild and one robust in flavour, might be chosen. Mild – Cheddar, Caerphilly, Lancashire, Double Gloucester, Red and White Leicester, White Stilton and White and Red Cheshire. Robust – Blue Stilton, Blue Cheshire, Sage Derby, Red Windsor. Add to these as a contrast a soft paste cheese (crushed peppercorns, chopped spring onion or capers beaten into curd cheese and seasoned with salt and pepper to taste). Place a small dish or pot of soft margarine or fairly soft butter on the board. (If the spread is hard it will break the biscuits.) Complete with a basket lined with a napkin and filled with a selection of hotel biscuits, cream crackers or water biscuits and crispbreads. To make a complete meal of the cheese course combined with soup or a sweet, add celery sticks, radishes, whole spring onions, pickled onions, piccalilli, pickled walnuts, sweet pickle, or a selection of fresh nuts.

CONTINENTAL CHEESE-BOARD

Try to keep the same country of origin for all the cheeses. A French semi-hard cheese such as Port Salut or Tome de Savoie; a soft crusted cheese such as Camembert, Brie or Pont l'Evêque; and a flavoured cream cheese of the Boursin type would make a good selection with sliced French bread. Italian Gorgonzola or Dolcelatte can be offered together with the milder Bel Paese and bread sticks or grissini rather than biscuits.

Sandwiches and Snacks

SUPER SANDWICHES

Adventurous snack meals can be made by combining original fillings with one or other of the many varieties of fresh bread now available.

Every-day Sandwiches

Use soft margarine or softened butter for spreading, preferably using sliced bread and preparing enough slices with spread before filling and putting together the sandwiches. To give sandwiches a lift, choose rye bread with caraway seeds, granary bread, bran or wheatgerm bread.

Fillings

Peanut butter mixed with crumbled crisply grilled bacon;
Cream cheese with chopped seedless raisins and spring onions;
Canned tuna or salmon mixed with mayonnaise and capers;
Any sliced cooked meat with chutney.

If crusts are to be removed, pile four sandwiches at a time into a stack and remove crusts with a very sharp knife. Wrap in foil or cling film to keep fresh until required, or for freezing. Allow 2 hours for a pack of wrapped frozen sandwiches to defrost, but the process can be hastened by separating them on a serving plate, lightly covered.

Danish Open Sandwiches

Use light or dark rye bread, well buttered.

Toppings

Liver pâté topped with lettuce heart and sliced canned button mushrooms;
Cold scrambled egg and canned ham topped with a gherkin fan;
Lettuce leaf cup filled with shrimps or prawns, piped rosette of mayonnaise and lemon slice;

Strips of pickled herring fillets with raw onion rings and tomato slices.

THREE-DECKER CLUB SANDWICHES

Use three slices of white bread or any bread suggested for every-day sandwiches for each club sandwich. Butter two of the slices of bread on one side only. Spread the third slice thinly with French mustard on both sides and use this for the centre layer.
Fillings
Sliced roast chicken or turkey + shredded lettuce in mayonnaise;
Thinly sliced smoked garlic sausage + tomato and cucumber slices;
Hard-boiled egg mashed with a little mayonnaise and a pinch of curry powder + watercress;
Sliced corned beef + coleslaw.

TOASTED SANDWICHES

Use two thin slices of white or wholemeal bread. Butter very lightly on both sides and make up the sandwiches.
Fillings
Sandwich 2 thin slices of Gouda cheese together with raw onion rings;
Lightly mashed banana seasoned with salt, pepper and lemon juice combined with a little mango chutney;
Chopped grilled bacon combined with fried sliced mushrooms and a little sweet brown pickle.
For a very simple toasted sandwich put a seasoned fried egg between two slices of buttered toast.

QUICK HOT SNACKS

Food from the storecupboard or delicatessen counter combine well with every-day ingredients like bread and potatoes to make quite substantial snack dishes, much more exciting than ordinary sandwiches.

Make a thick white sauce, flavour it with lemon juice, stir in flaked canned salmon or tuna and serve as a toast topper.

Make a poached egg more exciting by garnishing it with canned anchovies to give a fine lattice effect, or sprinkling with capers.

Make canned ham and mustard sandwiches, putting the butter-side outside. Toast under a hot grill, or fry them.

Slice hot dogs into homemade vegetable soup to make it more substantial.

Remove the centre from cooked jacket potatoes, mix with canned minced steak and onions and return to the oven to heat through.

Make fritters with canned pressed cod roe or luncheon meat by slicing it, dipping in a thick batter and deep frying.

Fill pastry squares with diced ham and liver pâté, make into turnovers and bake in the usual way.

To make a frying pan meal, cook sliced onion and potato with shredded cabbage in a little oil until soft. Add strips of garlic sausage and continue frying until brown.

Cut a small French loaf in half lengthways and then each half into four. Spread cut surfaces with tomato ketchup, a little grated cheese, strips of salami, then more grated cheese, and grill until golden brown.

Spread thinly rolled scone mixture with Ardennes or Provençal pâté or liver sausage, roll up like a Swiss roll, cut in thick slices and bake pinwheels as for scones.

Fruit

Fresh fruits are important to a healthy diet and fortunately there is now a much wider choice of imported fruit available all round the year. Citrus fruits, formerly restricted to oranges, grapefruits, lemons and tangerine varieties, now include many newcomers. Limes − similar to lemons but with green rind and distinctive lime flavour. Pink grapefruit − slightly sweeter flavour than an ordinary grapefruit but with pink flesh. Satsumas, Clementines etc. − cross-breds of the tangerine variety, some pipless and some especially easy to peel and segment. Particularly suited to eating straight from the fruit bowl. More exotic are Kiwi fruit − juicy green flesh under a downy brown skin, and Lichees − juicy white flesh under a prickly brown skin. Paw-paws and pomegranates have definite rinds and pips which must be discarded. The mango, somewhat similar, has a large stone. Melons − Water Melons, with green rind and pink flesh; Honeydew, Ogen, Charentais and Galia with green or golden rinds and flesh ranging from pale golden-green through golden-yellow to apricot when ripe. (All with pips which must be discarded.) Besides making exotic fruit salads combined with well-known favourites such as apples, pears, bananas and grapes, some are suitable for combination dishes, even savoury salads.

FRUIT FRITTERS

100 g (4 oz) plain flour
Pinch of salt
1 tablespoon oil
1 egg, separated
150 ml ($\frac{1}{4}$ pint) water

3 medium cooking
*   apples or 3 large*
*   bananas or 8 drained*
*   canned peach halves or*
*   pineapple rings*
Oil for deep frying

First make up the batter. Sift the flour and salt into a bowl then add the oil and egg yolk and half the water and whisk steadily, gradually drawing in the dry ingredients, until the batter is smooth. Whisk in the remaining water. Leave to stand for 15 minutes. Peel, core and slice the apples, halve the bananas and split each half lengthways, drain canned fruit really well on absorbent kitchen paper. Whisk the egg white until stiff. Whisk up the batter again and fold in the egg white. Dip pieces of fruit in the batter and fry in deep hot oil for 2–3 minutes, or until golden brown. Drain well and serve with sugar to sprinkle. Serves 4.

RHUBARB AND ORANGE COMPÔTE

0.75 kg (1½ lb) rhubarb,   *Finely grated rind and*
  trimmed   *juice of 2 oranges*
175 g (6 oz) castor sugar

Cut the rhubarb into 2.5 cm (1 inch) lengths and place in an ovenproof dish. Sprinkle with the sugar and pour over the orange rind and juice. Stir well. Cover the dish and cook in a moderate oven (160°C, 325°F, Gas Mark 3) for 35 minutes. Remove the dish from the oven and leave to stand, still covered, for 15 minutes before serving with cream or custard. Serves 4–6.

EXOTIC FRUIT SALAD

75 g (3 oz) sugar   *1 large orange, peeled*
1 tablespoon lemon juice   *and segmented*
150 ml (¼ pint) water   *1 large banana, sliced*
50 g (2 oz) fresh dates,   *100 g (4 oz) strawberries,*
  stoned and halved   *halved*
1 large dessert apple,
  cored and sliced

Place the sugar in a saucepan with the lemon juice and water and stir over gentle heat until dissolved. Boil vigorously for 1 minute then cool. Add the prepared fruit to the syrup. (If liked, also add 1 tablespoon sweet vermouth, Cointreau, or Kirsch.) Chill before serving with whipped cream.

Serves 4.

Note: Other combinations of fruits are just as enjoyable but try to include contrasts of colours and textures.

Variations:

Quick Fruit Salad — Start with a 225 g (8 oz) can of apricot halves, peach slices or pineapple pieces. Add 2 other prepared fruits of your choice and 8 cocktail cherries. Chill and serve with canned cream.

Pineapple Cup Salads — When small pineapples are in season, this is an inexpensive spectacular dessert. Cut 2 small pineapples in half lengthways, right through the leafy part. Scoop out the flesh using a grapefruit knife, taking care not to waste any of the juice. Discard the woody core, dice the remaining flesh and combine with other prepared fruits of your choice and the juice. Sprinkle with sugar, cover and chill for at least 1 hour. Serve the fruit salad piled up in the pineapple cups.

KIWI NUT SALAD

2 kiwi fruit	2 tablespoons sauce
1 orange	vinaigrette*
1 banana	4 lettuce leaves,
1 stick celery	shredded
5 cm (2 inch) length	25 g (1 oz) cashews or
cucumber	roasted peanuts

Peel the kiwi fruit and slice the flesh. Peel the orange, removing all pith. Cut into thin slices and cut each slice into quarters. Slice the banana thickly, cut the celery into very thin slivers and dice the cucumber. Place the sauce vinaigrette in the base of a salad bowl, arrange the pieces of orange in the bowl then cover with the remaining ingredients. Toss the salad with the dressing at serving time.

Serves 4.

TIPSY STRAWBERRIES IN CREAM

450 g (1 lb) firm
  strawberries
2 tablespoons castor
  sugar

2 tablespoons Kirsch or
  Cointreau
300 ml ($\frac{1}{2}$ pint) double
  cream

Slice the strawberries into a bowl, sprinkle over the sugar and
liqueur. Chill for 2 hours. Whip the cream until thick and
almost stiff then fold in the strawberries and syrup. Turn into 6
glass serving dishes and serve immediately.
Serves 6.

BLACKCURRANT SOUFFLÉ

450 g (1 lb) blackcurrants
Granulated sugar
4 teaspoons gelatine
3 tablespoons water
4 eggs, separated

50 g (2 oz) castor sugar
150 ml ($\frac{1}{4}$ pint) double
  cream
50 g (2 oz) chopped
  toasted almonds

Place the blackcurrants in a pan with 150 ml ($\frac{1}{4}$ pint) water and
cook gently for about 15 minutes, or until soft. Press through a
sieve to give 300 ml ($\frac{1}{2}$ pint) purée. (If the amount of purée pro-
duced is much over this quantity, return it to the saucepan and
boil rapidly until reduced.) Sweeten to taste with granulated
sugar and cool. Prepare a 17.5 cm (7 inch) soufflé dish by tying a
double thickness of greaseproof paper or foil round the top edge,
to come about 5 cm (2 inches) above the top of the dish. Dissolve
the gelatine in the water in a basin over a pan of hot water. Cool.
Place the egg yolks and castor sugar in a basin and whisk with an
electric mixer until pale and thick. If whisking by hand, it is
necessary to place the basin over a pan of hot water then remove
from the heat and continue whisking until cold. Whisk in the
fruit purée and dissolved gelatine. Whip the cream until thick
and whisk the egg whites until stiff. Fold these gently into the
fruit mixture until completely blended. Turn into the prepared
dish and chill until set. At serving time, carefully remove the
band of paper and press the nuts against the exposed sides of the
soufflé.

Serves 4–6.

Variation:

Raspberry Soufflé – Press 350 g (12 oz) raspberries through a sieve and sweeten the purée with icing sugar. Use in place of the blackcurrant purée.

LEMON AND LIME SORBET

Pared rind and juice of
  2 lemons
Pared rind and juice of
  2 limes

900 ml (1 $\frac{1}{2}$ pints) water
About 200 g (7 oz) sugar
1 tablespoon gelatine
1 small egg white

Put the fruit rinds and juices, the water and sugar into a saucepan and stir over gentle heat until the sugar has dissolved. Bring to the boil then allow to bubble gently for 10 minutes. Strain the liquid into a jug, add extra sugar if necessary and allow to cool. Dissolve the gelatine in 2 tablespoons water in a basin over a pan of hot water. Cool and stir into the lemon liquid. Turn into a shallow container and freeze until mushy. Turn into a bowl and beat until smooth. Whisk the egg white and when stiff, fold thoroughly into the lemon mixture. Return to the container and freeze until firm. Turn out again and beat until smooth then return to the container and freeze. Serve the sorbet scooped into stemmed glasses.

Serves 4–6.

Variation:

Lemon and Orange Sorbet – Use the rind and juice of 3 oranges and 1 lemon instead of the lemons and limes but reduce the sugar to about 100 g (4 oz).

EASY-SET STRAWBERRY AND RHUBARB JAM

450 g (1 lb) trimmed
  rhubarb
4 tablespoons water
3 tablespoons lemon
  juice

0.5 kg (1 $\frac{1}{4}$ lb) small
  strawberries
1.5 kg (3 lb) sugar
$\frac{1}{2}$ bottle commercial
  fruit pectin

Finely chop the rhubarb and place in a large pan with the water and lemon juice. Bring to the boil then simmer for 5 minutes, or until the fruit is tender. Add the strawberries and sugar and heat gently, stirring occasionally, until the sugar has completely dissolved. Bring to a full rolling boil and leave to cook rapidly for 3 minutes from this point. Remove from the heat and stir in the pectin thoroughly. Leave the jam to cool, stir well to distribute the fruit, then turn into clean, dry and warm pots, cover, seal tightly and label.

Makes about 2.25 kg (5 lb).

ORANGE JELLY MARMALADE

4 *sweet oranges*	4.5 *litres (8 pints)*
4 *Seville oranges*	*water*
2 *lemons*	*Sugar*

Slice the oranges and lemons thinly. Remove the pips and tie them in a piece of muslin. Place the fruit and bag of pips in a preserving pan with the water and bring to the boil. Simmer for about $3\frac{1}{2}$ hours, or until the liquid has reduced by half. Strain through a jelly bag overnight then measure the juice and allow 450 g (1 lb) sugar to each 600 ml (1 pint). Return the juice to the pan with the sugar and heat gently, stirring occasionally, until the sugar has completely dissolved. Bring to a full rolling boil and continue boiling rapidly until setting point is reached. To test for setting, spoon a little syrup on to a cold plate, allow to cool and draw a fingertip through the centre. The jelly should separate into two distinct parts. Remove the pan from the heat while testing for setting point, otherwise it may overcook. Turn the marmalade into clean, dry and warm pots while still hot, cover, seal tightly and label.

Makes about 1.75 kg (4 lb).

GREEN TOMATO CHUTNEY

1.5 *kg (3 lb) green*	225 *g (8 oz) onions,*
tomatoes, quartered	*chopped*

166

2 tablespoons salt
100 g (4 oz) tenderised
  prunes
225 g (8 oz) dessert
  apples
100 g (4 oz) pressed
  dates, chopped

350 g (12 oz) soft brown
  sugar
600 ml (1 pint) malt
  vinegar
2 teaspoons mustard
  seeds
1 teaspoon mixed pickling
  spices

Remove the hard stalk ends from the pieces of tomato then chop roughly and place in a preserving pan and sprinkle over the salt. Soak the prunes in cold water to cover. Leave the tomatoes and prunes overnight. Drain the liquid from the tomatoes. Drain and stone the prunes. Peel, core and chop the apples and add to the tomato with the prunes, dates, onion, sugar and vinegar. Tie the mustard seeds and pickling spices in a piece of muslin and add to the pan. Heat gently, stirring frequently, until the sugar has dissolved then bring to the boil and simmer for $1\frac{1}{2}$ –2 hours, or until the chutney is reduced to a soft thick pulp. Remove the bag of spices. Turn into clean, dry and warm jars, cover, seal tightly and label.

Makes about 1.75 kg (4 lb).

Drinks

TEA

Making good tea is easy. The rules include using freshly boiled water, a warm dry pot, the equivalent of one teaspoon of tea per person (and one for the pot if a second cup is needed). Count each teabag as 1 teaspoon. Stir the brew before you put on the lid, and if using loose tea, pour out through a strainer. Allow to stand a minimum of 2 minutes first. Add milk to the cups before pouring in the tea.

ICED TEA: Have ready plenty of ice. Make the tea double strength. Put sugar, if required, into tall glasses. Add lemon juice if liked, and stir in sufficient freshly-made hot tea to fill one third of each glass. Stir well, add ice to fill the glasses and top each with a slice of fresh lemon.

COFFEE

Making good coffee depends a great deal on the freshness of the coffee beans and on using the correct grind of coffee for the method. Buy it roasted, but grind your own as required if you can. Suit the grind to the method of making; coarse for the jug method, finer for percolators or electric coffee makers requiring filters. The makers of these pieces of equipment always indicate the correct grind to use. Add cold milk or cream to taste. Hot milk alters the flavour.

ICED COFFEE: Have ready plenty of ice. Make the coffee double strength. Put sugar, if required, in the bottom of a tall glass, stir in sufficient freshly-made hot coffee to fill one third of the glass. Stir well. Either add cold milk to fill the second third of the glass, then top up with ice and stir well. (To make very rich iced coffee, use part cream.) Alternatively, use a little more coffee, then add scoops of vanilla ice cream to fill the glass.

GAELIC COFFEE: Use special glasses with handles, or Paris goblets. Put at least 2 teaspoons of sugar in the bottom of each glass, add 1 tablespoon Scotch whisky or Irish whiskey, and stir well. Fill up to within 2.5 cm (1 inch) of the top of the glass with hot coffee, stirring all the time. Pour in lightly whipped whipping cream or unwhipped double cream over the back of a cold teaspoon, very slowly so that it does not sink into the coffee. Fill almost to the tops of the glasses.

GLÜHWEIN

Grated rind and juice of
1 lemon
100 g (4 oz) sugar
6 cloves

$\frac{1}{2}$ *cinnamon stick*
300 ml ($\frac{1}{2}$ pint) water
2 1 litre (35.2 fl oz)
bottles red wine

Place the lemon rind, sugar, cloves and cinnamon stick in a pan with the water and bring to the boil. Remove from the heat and leave to stand for 30 minutes. Strain the syrup into a large clean saucepan and add the wine. Heat until just below boiling point then stir in the lemon juice and serve hot in small glasses. Makes about 15 small glasses.

SANGRIA

225 g (8 oz) sugar
300 ml ($\frac{1}{2}$ pint) water
1 stick of cinnamon or
1 teaspoon ground
cinnamon
3 oranges
2 lemons

About 24 ice cubes
1 bottle red wine
4 tablespoons white rum
or any fruit liqueur
900 ml (1 $\frac{1}{2}$ pints) soda
water

Dissolve the sugar in the water in a saucepan. Add the cinnamon and boil for 5 minutes. Cool. Slice the oranges and lemons into a large bowl and strain the syrup over them. Leave to stand for 4 hours. Crush the ice, add to the bowl with the wine and spirit and stir well. Finally add the soda water and serve in chilled wine glasses.

Makes about 15 small glasses.

TYPE OF JOINT	ROASTING TIME AT	ROASTING TIME AT
BEEF on the bone	220°C, 425°F, Gas 7 20 minutes per 450 g (1 lb) plus 20 minutes.	190°C, 375°F, Gas 5 27 minutes per 450 g (1 lb) plus 27 minutes.
boned and rolled (including stuffing)	25 minutes per 450 g (1 lb) plus 25 minutes.	33 minutes per 450 g (1 lb) plus 33 minutes.
PORK on the bone	25 minutes per 450 g (1 lb) plus 25 minutes.	30 minutes per 450 g (1 lb) plus 30 minutes.
boned and rolled (including stuffing)	not recommended	35 minutes per 450 g (1 lb) plus 35 minutes.
LAMB on the bone	20 minutes per 450 g (1 lb) plus 20 minutes.	at 180°C, 350°F, Gas 4, 35 minutes per 450 g (1 lb).
boned and rolled (including stuffing)	25 minutes per 450 g (1 lb) plus 25 minutes.	at 180°C, 350°F, Gas 4, 45 minutes per 450 g (1 lb).
TURKEY whole bird (including stuffing) 2.75–3.5 kg (6–8 lb) 4–5.5 kg (9–12 lb)	at 190°C, 375°F, Gas 5, $2\frac{1}{2}$ –3 hours 3–3$\frac{1}{2}$ hours	at 160°C, 325°F, Gas 3, 3–3$\frac{1}{2}$ hours 3$\frac{1}{2}$ –4 hours
CHICKEN whole bird (including stuffing)	at 200°C, 400°F, Gas 6, 20 minutes per 450 g (1 lb) plus	at 180°C, 350°F, Gas 4, 25 minutes per 450 g (1 lb) plus
DUCK whole bird (including stuffing) on a rack	20 minutes. at 200°C, 400°F, Gas 6, 15 minutes per 450 g (1 lb) plus 15 minutes.	25 minutes.

Note: Joints or whole birds covered with foil require slightly longer cooking time.
Open foil for the last 20 minutes to encourage browning.

INDEX

176

182

DR. ATKIN'S SUPER ENERGY DIET
by DR. ROBERT C. ATKINS
   SHIRLEY LINDE

The diet revolution answer to Fatigue and depression.

Dr. Atkins has done it again! The physician whose bestselling Dr. Atkin's Diet Revolution helped thousands upon thousands of people to lose weight now does for fatigue and depression what he did so successfully for excess pounds. Now, he offers his personally tested program to help you feel better than you ever have before. How? With four, easy-to-follow, good-eating, no-hunger diets:

THE SUPERENERGY WEIGHT REDUCING DIET for those who want to lose weight as well as gain energy.

THE SUPERENERGY WEIGHT GAINING DIET for those who want to gain weight and more energy.

THE SUPERENERGY WEIGHT MAINTENANCE DIET for those who want to keep their weight the same, and to enjoy superenergy.

THE SPECIAL SITUATION DIET for those under medical supervision who are pregnant, facing surgery, on special medication or need more carbohydrates.

One of these diets may be right for you. Glowing vibrant health can be yours. Isn't it worth a try? Start today.

0 552 11033 7   £1.25

DR. ATKIN'S DIET COOKBOOK
by FRAN GARE & HELEN MONICA

We all want to be slim and healthy — but one of the greatest drawbacks to dieting is the boredom of living on those low-calorie foods. Now Bantam have published an eat-well-and-keep-slim cookbook based on DR. ATKIN'S DIET REVOLUTION and written under the doctor's supervision. An indispensable guide to variety which will keep dieters' boredom at bay.

0 552 14888 5   £1.25

THE 'I HATE TO HOUSEKEEP' BOOK
by PEG BRACKEN

This companion volume to The 'I Hate to Cook' Book will add sunshine to your smile and sparkle to your woodwork. Even if you don't have to keep house you will enjoy it.

It tells you, among hundreds of other useful things—
How to be tightfisted without having it show.
How to remember, and how to remember to remember.
How to be happy when you're absolutely miserable.

And many hints and wrinkles you have never even thought of!

0 552 106070 65p

THE CHICKEN COOKBOOK
by ANNE MASON

An invaluable, comprehensive and popular collection of chicken recipes from around the world — together with everything you need to know about buying, freezing and preparing.

Crammed with fascinating ideas for simple and sophisticated dishes, from Kentish Pie to Provencal Casserole, from soup to Pate, and from Glazed to Drunken Chicken. Eat it Viennese or Somerset style. Prepare it as they do in Cheshire, Scotland or Crete.

All the chicken recipes in the world in one book!

0 55 98099 4 £1.25

THE SCOTTISH COOKERY BOOK
by ELIZABETH CRAIG

IF YOU WANT TO GET THE REAL FLAVOUR OF
SCOTTISH COOKING, HERE IS THE BOOK

A really comprehensive collection of Scottish recipes which
should appeal to both the experienced and the inexperienced
cook.

Scottish fare is essentially wholesome — good plain meat
and fish dishes, breads and teacakes, and, of course, the
earthy haggis. But there is sophistication and glamour too.
The Auld Alliance left behind a legacy of French delicacy
which flavours many of the recipes, and some of the titles
make the Sassenach's mouth water and the soul of the
Scotsman swell: add 4 dessertspoons of liquid heather

honey, eat Venus Puddin', Roastit Bubbly-jock or Sole wi'
a Delicate Air.

Contents include:

Soups* Fish*
Sandwiches* Eggs
Puddin's and Pipes
Sauces* Vegetables
Meat* Game and Poultry
Savouries* Breads, Scones
and Teabread* Biscuits
Beverages* Candies
Preserves.

0 552 98087 0 £1.95

A SELECTED LIST OF TITLES
PUBLISHED BY CORGI BOOKS

WHILE EVERY EFFORT IS MADE TO KEEP PRICES LOW, IT IS SOMETIMES
NECESSARY TO INCREASE PRICES AT SHORT NOTICE. CORGI BOOKS RESERVE
THE RIGHT TO SHOW NEW RETAIL PRICES ON COVERS WHICH MAY DIFFER FROM
THOSE PREVIOUSLY ADVERTISED IN THE TEXT OR ELSEWHERE.

THE PRICES SHOWN BELOW WERE CORRECT AT THE TIME OF GOING TO PRESS
(MAY '82).

ORDER FORM

All these books are available at your bookshop or newsagent, or can be ordered direct from the publisher. Just tick the titles you want and fill in the form below.

CORGI BOOKS, Cash Sales Department, P.O. Box 11, Falmouth, Cornwall.

Please send cheque or postal order, no currency.

Please allow cost of book(s) plus the following for postage and packing:

U.K. Customers Allow 45p for the first book, 20p for the second book and 14p for each additional
book ordered, to a maximum charge of £1.63.

B.F.P.O. and Eire Allow 45p for the first book, 20p for the second book plus 14p per copy for the
next 7 books, thereafter 8p per book.

Overseas Customers - Allow 75p for the first book and 21p per copy for each additional book.

NAME (Block Letters) ....

ADDRESS ....

....

(MAY '82) ....